VOGUE® KNITTING

CROCHETED
HATS

VOGUE KNITTING
CROCHETED HATS

SIXTH&SPRING BOOKS
NEW YORK

SIXTH&SPRING BOOKS
233 Spring Street
New York, New York 10013

Library of Congress Cataloging-in-Publication Data

Library of Congress Control Number: 2005926331

ISBN: 1-931543-78-X
ISBN-13: 978-1-931543-78-1

Manufactured in China

5 7 9 10 8 6 4

First Edition

TABLE OF CONTENTS

INTRODUCTION

Maybe you were first drawn to this book because you've searched far and wide in vain for a store-bought hat to match that delightfully peculiar shade of pea green in your new coat. Or you live in Alaska and your ears always get cold. Or you just have a lot of bad hair days. All are respectable motives—and doubtless the inspirations for countless other crocheted caps throughout history.

But we had a crazy thought: What if stitching a hat didn't have to be so hopelessly practical? Thanks to the availability of gorgeous new yarns in unique textures and vivid colors, hats no longer have to be just an afterthought. They can actually make an outfit, dressing it up or down, transforming it from forgettable to fabulous, or simply providing the perfect finishing touch. And with a prominent place atop your head, they're the ultimate way to flaunt your personal flair.

Equal parts function and fashion, this newest "On the go!" collection has something for every person and personality, with hip, fresh designs that breathe new life into classic looks and translate the latest styles into easy-to-follow patterns. Try the beanie or mesh cap for a contemporary look, or go vintage with the mini ruffle pillbox or feminine mohair flower cloche. Whether you're a veteran crocheter or a newbie, you'll find something to suit your skill level. The best part? These projects work up quickly and are small enough to take with you anywhere.

So grab your hook and yarn, start from the top, and CROCHET ON THE GO!

THE BASICS

These days, the word is that crochet has made a comeback; history, though, tells us it never really left. People are just exploring new hobbies, rediscovering old skills and expanding their knowledge of handcrafts. Our aim is to encourage and entice a whole spectrum of crocheters, whatever their experience, with this book.

Crochet is accessible and really quite easy to learn. Stitches are formed by pulling loops through other loops or stitches with a hook, creating a simple chain that is used in all patterns. Unlike knitting, there is no balancing act with stitches, shifting them from one needle to another; in crochet, one hand does all the work, and finished fabric lays away from the hook, letting crocheters concentrate on only the newest stitch they need to make. Also, since the stitches are not attached to needles, it's easy to custom-fit as you work, something that's very difficult to do when you're knitting. Unlike other crafts, correcting a mistake is fairly stress free—simply tug on the yarn to easily pull out the stitches you have worked.

If you're not convinced that it's easy to learn to crochet, perhaps the hats and caps in this collection will inspire you. They run the gamut from the most basic stitches to more complicated ones, giving experienced crocheters ample selection and offering novices the chance to graduate to more difficult projects as they progress. The beginner styles, such as the Tweed Hat on page 21 and the Mesh Cap on page 36, use basic stitches and minimal shaping. Meanwhile, the more advanced designs, like the Quilted Effect hat on page 39, do not necessarily have more difficult stitch techniques; rather the instructions, with their series of repeats and pattern layouts, require more concentration to create the perfect piece.

TYPES OF CAPS AND HATS

Caps

A cap is a snug-fitting hat that fits closely to the head. The finished circumference of these styles will be smaller than your actual head measurement. Caps are also usually worn above or just covering the ears. These simple styles are among the easiest to knit.

Caps in this collection include the Striped Cap on page 33 with its openwork design, the multi-colored Kilim Cap on page 50 and the highly-textured Beehive Hat on page 54.

Berets

Berets are flat caps, often topped with a pom-pom or tassels. The Mitred Beret on page 80 has an interesting construction. Single crochet squares are arranged on the top of the hat with triangle shapes in the corners to form a circle. A ribbed band (made of single crochet, worked in the back loops only) gives the hat a good fit.

Brimmed Hats

These styles flatter the face and exude an air of sophistication, and they are influenced by traditional millinery techniques. Examples of brimmed hats in this collection are the Bobbled Cloche on page 44 and the Classic Cloche on page 86.

Helmets, Toques and Pillboxes

These styles sport flat or slightly rounded tops with straight sides. They sit fairly high on the head and utilize a special millinery-inspired rolled trim. The flat tops are achieved by decreases worked in slanting or spiral patterns. The Mini Ruffle Pillbox Hat on page 27 and the Striped Helmet on page 47 exemplify these styles.

YARN SELECTION

For an exact reproduction of the hat photographed, use the yarn listed in the

SIZING

Most of the hats and caps in this book are sized for women. Those suitable for men and children are indicated in the sizes section of the instructions.

To avoid making a hat that is too tight, measure for head size before you begin to knit. Sizing is particularly important for structured hat styles. To measure, place a tape measure across the forehead and measure around the full circumference of the head. Keep the tape snug for accurate results.

All the hats in the book are given a fit category: very loose-fitting, loose-fitting, standard-fitting, close-fitting and very close-fitting. To change the fit of your hat or cap style, you can experiment with needles sized smaller (for a closer fit) or larger (for a looser fit). Or you may wish to eliminate rows or pattern bands for a style with less depth, or add rows or bands for a deeper hat style.

Head sizes used in this book		
SIZE	INCHES	CM
X-Small	20	51
Small	21	53
Medium	22	56
Large	23	59

materials section of the pattern. We've selected yarns that are readily available in the U.S. and Canada at the time of printing. The Resources list on page 92 provides addresses of yarn distributors. Contact them for the name of a retailer in your area.

YARN SUBSTITUTION
You may wish to substitute yarns. Perhaps a spectacular yarn matches your new coat; maybe you view small-scale projects as a chance to incorporate leftovers from your yarn stash; or it may be that the yarn specified is not available in your area. Hats allow you to be as creative as you like, but you'll need to crochet to the given gauge to obtain the finished measurements with the substitute yarn. Make pattern adjustments where necessary. Be sure to consider how different yarn types (chenille, mohair, bouclé, etc.) will affect the final appearance of your hat. Also take fiber care into consideration: Some yarns can be machine- or hand-washed; others will require dry cleaning.

To facilitate yarn substitution, Vogue Knitting grades yarn by the standard stitch gauge obtained in single crochet. You'll find a grading number in the "Materials" section of the pattern, immediately following the yarn information. Look for a substitute yarn that falls into the same category. The suggested hook size and gauge on the ball band should be comparable to that on the Standard Yarn Weight chart on page 13.

After you've successfully gauge-swatched a substitute yarn, you'll need to figure out how much of the substitute yarn the project requires. First, find the total length of the original yarn in the pattern (multiply number of balls by yards/meters per ball). Divide this figure by the new yards/meters per ball (listed on the ball band). Round up to the next whole number. The answer is the number of balls required.

READING CROCHET INSTRUCTIONS

If you are used to reading knitting instructions, then crochet instructions may seem a little tedious to follow. This is because crochet instructions use more abbreviations and punctuations and fewer words than traditional knitting instructions. Along with the separation of stitches and use of brackets, parentheses, commas and other punctuation, there are numerous repetitions going on within a single row or round. Therefore, you must pay closer attention to reading instructions while you crochet. Here are a few explanations of the more common terminology used in this book.

Use of Parentheses ( )
Sometimes parentheses will be used to indicate the stitches that will be worked all into one stitch such as "in next st work ( )" or "( ) in next st."

Categories of yarn, gauge ranges and recommended needle and hook sizes

Yarn Weight Symbol & Category Names	1 Super Fine	2 Fine	3 Light	4 Medium	5 Bulky	6 Super Bulky
Type of Yarns in Category	Sock, Fingering, Baby	Sport, Baby	DK, Light Worsted	Worsted, Afghan, Aran	Chunky, Craft, Rug	Bulky, Roving
Crochet Gauge Ranges in Single Crochet to 4 inch	21–32 sts	16–20 sts	12–17 sts	11–14 sts	8–11 sts	5–9 sts
Recommended Hook U.S. Size Range	B–1 to E–4	E–4 to 7	7 to I–9	I–9 to K–10½	K–10½ to M–13	M–13 and larger
Recommended Hook in Metric Size Range	2.25–3.5 mm	3.5–4.5 mm	4.5–5.5 mm	5.5–6.5 mm	6.5–9 mm	9–12 mm and larger

* GUIDELINES ONLY: The above reflect the most commonly used gauges and needle or hook sizes for specific yarn categories.

*Guidelines only: The above reflects the most commonly used needle or hook sizes for specific yarn categories.

U.S.	Metric
14 steel	.60mm
12 steel	.75mm
10 steel	1.00mm
6 steel	1.50mm
5 steel	1.75mm
B/1	2.00mm
U.S.	Metric
C/2	2.50mm
D/3	3.00mm
E/4	3.50mm
F/5	4.00mm
G/6	4.50mm
H/8	5.00mm
U.S.	Metric
I/9	5.50mm
J/10	6.00mm
	6.50mm
K/10.5	7.00mm

SKILL LEVELS FOR CROCHET

BEGINNER
Ideal first project.

VERY EASY VERY VOGUE
Basic stitches, minimal shaping, simple finishing.

INTERMEDIATE
For crocheters with some experience.
More intricate stitches, shaping and finishing.

EXPERIENCED
For crocheters able to work patterns with complicated shaping and finishing.

Getting the correct gauge is essential to crocheting a garment that's the correct size. The gauge is the number of stitches (measured horizontally) and rows (measured vertically) you need to get over a span of usually 4"/10cm square in a specified pattern stitch, using the yarn and crochet hook size called for in the materials list. The number of stitches to the inch/centimeter (or gauge) dictates how many stitches will be crocheted to achieve the finished measurements.

Making a gauge swatch enables you to achieve the recommended gauge before you begin your project. With the same yarn and crochet hook size called for in the directions, chain sufficient stitches for a 5"/12.5cm-wide swatch, then work in the pattern stitch specified in the directions for 5"/12.5cm. Do not fasten off. Place the swatch on a hard, flat surface. For stitches across, place a ruler or stitch gauge

(pictured here) horizontally on the swatch. Position the 1"/2.5cm mark even with a whole stitch, then working toward the right count 4"/10cm worth of stitches. If you have more stitches to the inch/centimeter than is recommended, remake the swatch using a hook that's one size larger. If you have fewer stitches than stated, try again with a smaller hook. The same applies for measuring the row gauge, except position the ruler vertically.

First st, Next st

The beginning stitch of every row is referred to as the "first st." When counting the turning chain (t-ch) as one stitch, the row or round will begin by stating to work into the next st (that is, skip the first st or space or whatever is designated in the pattern).

Stitch Counts

Sometimes the turning chain that is

worked at the end (or beginning) of a row or a round will be referred to as 1 stitch and then is counted in the stitch count. When the t-ch is counted as 1 stitch, you will work into the next stitch, thus skipping the first stitch of the row or round. When the t-ch is not counted as a stitch, work into the first stitch.

Stitches Described

Sometimes the stitches are described as

sc, dc, tr, ch-2 loop, 2-dc group, etc. and sometimes—such as in a mesh pattern of sc, ch 1—each sc and each ch 1 will be referred to as a st.

Back Loop

Along the top of each crochet stitch or chain there are two loops. The loop furthest away from you is the "back loop."

Front Loop

Along the top of each crochet stitch or chain there are two loops. The loop closest to you is the "front loop."

Joining New Colors

When joining new colors in crochet, whether at the beginning of a row or while working across, always work the stitch in the old color to the last 2 loops, then draw the new color through the 2 loops and continue with the new color.

Working Over Ends

Crochet has a unique flat top along each row that is perfect for laying the old color across and working over the ends for several stitches. This will alleviate the cutting and weaving in of ends later.

Form a Ring

When a pattern is worked in the round, as in a square or medallion, the beginning chains are usually closed into a ring by working a slip stitch into the first chain. Then on the first round, stitches are usually worked into the ring and less often into each chain.

Refer to the yarn label for the recommended cleaning method. Many of the scarves in the book can be washed by hand (or in the machine on a gentle or wool cycle) in lukewarm water with a mild detergent. Do not agitate, and don't soak for more than 10 minutes. Rinse gently with tepid water, then fold in a towel and gently press the water out. Lay flat to dry, away from excessive heat and light.

FRINGE AND TASSELS

Cut yarn twice desired length of fringe plus extra for knotting. On wrong side, insert hook from front to back through piece and over folded yarn. Pull yarn through. Draw ends through and tighten. Trim yarn.

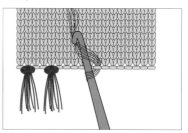

Cut a piece of cardboard to the desired length of the tassel. Wrap yarn around the cardboard. Knot a piece of yarn tightly around one end, cut as shown, and remove the cardboard. Wrap and tie yarn around the tassel about 1"/2.5cm down from the top to secure the fringe.

CHAIN

1 *Pass the yarn over the hook and catch it with the hook.*

2 *Draw the yarn through the loop on the hook.*

3 *Repeat steps 1 and 2 to make a chain.*

SINGLE CROCHET

1 *Insert the hook through top two loops of a stitch. Pass the yarn over the hook and draw up a loop—two loops on hook.*

2 *Pass the yarn over the hook and draw through both loops on hook.*

3 *Continue in the same way, inserting the hook into each stitch.*

HALF-DOUBLE CROCHET

1 *Pass the yarn over the hook. Insert the hook through the top two loops of a stitch.*

2 *Pass the yarn over the hook and draw up a loop—three loops on hook. Pass the yarn over the hook.*

3 *Draw through all three loops on hook.*

DOUBLE CROCHET

1 *Pass the yarn over the hook. Insert the hook through the top two loops of a stitch.*

2 *Pass the yarn over the hook and draw up a loop— three loops on hook.*

3 *Pass the yarn over the hook and draw it through the first two loops on the hook, pass the yarn over the hook and draw through the remaining two loops. Continue in the same way, inserting the hook into each stitch.*

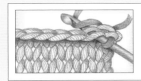

SLIP STITCH

Insert the crochet hook into a stitch, catch the yarn, and pull up a loop. Draw the loop through the loop on the hook.

CROCHET TERMS AND ABBREVIATIONS

approx approximately

beg begin(ning)

CC contrast color

ch chain(s)

cm centimeter(s)

cont continue(ing)

dc double crochet (UK: tr-treble)

dec decrease(ing)–Reduce the stitches in a row (work stitches together or skip the stitches).

foll follow(s)(ing)

g gram(s)

hdc half double crochet (UK: htr-half treble)

inc increase(ing)–Add stitches in a row (work extra stitches into a stitch or between the stitches).

LH left-hand

lp(s) loop(s)

m meter(s)

MC main color

mm millimeter(s)

oz ounce(s)

pat(s) pattern

pm place markers–Place or attach a loop of contrast yarn or purchased stitch marker as indicated.

rem remain(s)(ing)

rep repeat

rnd(s) round(s)

RH right-hand

RS right side(s)

sc single crochet (UK: dc-double crochet)

sk skip

sl st slip stitch (UK: sc-single crochet)

sp(s) space(s)

st(s) stitch(es)

t-ch turning chain

tog together

tr treble (UK: tr tr-triple treble)

WS wrong side(s)

work even Continue in pattern without increasing or decreasing. (UK: work straight)

yd yard(s)

yo yarn over–wrap the yarn around the hook (UK: yrh)

* = repeat directions following * as many times as indicated.

[ ] = Repeat directions inside brackets as many times as indicated.

Deep bands of faux fur trim this trapper-style helmet worked in a multicolor bouclé yarn. The front fur flap folds up and fur tassels form the tie ends in this design by Traci Bunkers.

SIZES

Instructions are written for one size.

KNITTED MEASUREMENTS

- Head circumference 21½"/54.5cm
- Depth 9"/23cm

MATERIALS

- 2 2½oz/70g balls (each approx 57yd/52m) of Lion Brand Yarn *Lion Bouclé* (acrylic/mohair/nylon) in #212 red multi (A) 5
- 3 1¾oz/50g balls (each approx 64yd/58m) of Fun Fur (polyester) in #113 red (B) 5
- Size N/13 (9mm) 5 crochet hook *or size to obtain gauge*

GAUGES

- 8 sc and 8 rows/rnds to 4"/10cm over sc pat st using 1 strand A and size N/13 (9mm) crochet hook.
- 9 sc and 9 rows to 4"/10cm over sc pat st using 2 strands B and size N/13 (9mm) crochet hook. *Take time to check gauges.*

STITCH GLOSSARY

Dec 1 sc

Insert hook in next st, yo and draw up a loop, insert hook in next st, yo and draw up a loop, yo and pull through all 3 loops on hook.

HELMET

Beg at lower edge with 1 strand each A and B held tog, loosely ch 43. Join with sl st to first ch, being careful not to twist ch.

Rnd 1 Ch 1, work 1 sc in each ch around—43 sc. Join and ch 1.

Rnds 2 and 3 Rep rnd 1.

Cut B and cont with A only, work in rnds of sc until piece measures 6"/15cm from beg.

CROWN SHAPING

Rnd 1 Work 1 sc, *dec 1 sc, sc in each of next 2 sts; rep from * to last 2 sts, 1 sc in each of last 2 sts—33 sc. Join and ch 1.

Rnd 2 Work 1 sc, *dec 1 sc, sc in each of next 2 sts; rep from* around—25 sc. Join and ch 1.

Rnd 3 Work 1 sc, *dec 1 sc, sc in next sc; rep from * around—17 sc. Join and ch 1.

Rnd 4 Work 1 sc, *dec 1 sc; rep from * around—9 sc. Join and ch 1.

Rnd 5 Rep rnd 4—5 sc. Cut yarn leaving a long end. Pull yarn through the sts at top and draw up tightly. Fasten off.

EAR FLAPS

Along the lower edge, place one marker, then a 2nd marker at a 5"/12.5cm interval to mark position of one earflap. With 2 strands B, join at the marker.

Row 1 (RS) Ch 1, work 11 sc to 2nd marker, ch 1, turn.

Work even in sc on 11 sc until earflap measures 5"/12.5cm

Dec row [Dec 1 sc] twice, 1 sc in each of next 3 sc, [dec 1 sc] twice—7 sc. Ch 1, turn.

Next row Dec 1 sc, 1 sc in each of next 3 sc, dec 1 sc—5 sc. Ch 1, turn.

Next row Dec 1 sc, 1 sc in next sc, dec 1 sc—3 sc. Cut B. With A yo and draw through all 3 sts on hook. Ch 30 for tie and fasten off, leaving a tail.

Front brim flap

Join 2 strands B just after the first earflap.

Row 1 (RS) Ch 1, work 15 sc evenly across. Ch 1, turn.

Work even in sc on 15 sc for 5"/12.5cm. Fasten off. Fold up brim and tack along top edge to helmet.

Work a 2nd ear flap on other side of brim flap.

TASSELS

(make 2)

Wrap B 20 times around a 4½"/11.5cm piece of cardboard. Tie top end of strands firmly and cut lower end. Wind yarn several times around the top of tassel at 1"/2.5cm from top. Attach tassels to ties.

TWEED HAT
Retro fitted

Two separate multicolor tweed yarns are held together to form this easy-to-crochet soft structure hat. The crown is edged with a top welt in this design by Kathy Merrick.

SIZES

Instructions are written for one size.

KNITTED MEASUREMENTS

- Head circumference 21"/53cm
- Depth 9"/23cm

MATERIALS

- 2 1¾oz/50g skeins (each approx 176yd/162m) of Koigu Wool Designs *Koigu Painters Palette Premium Merino* (wool) each in #324 (A) and #608 (B) **3**
- Size E/4 (3.5mm) crochet hook *or size to obtain gauge*

GAUGE

18 sc and 22 rows/rnds to 4"/10cm over sc pat using 2 strands (A and B) held tog and size E/4 (3.5mm) crochet hook. *Take time to check gauge.*

Note Hat is worked with 1 strand A and B held tog throughout.

HAT

Beg at crown edge, with 1 strand A and B held tog, ch 4, join with sl st to form ring.

Rnd 1 Work 8 sc into ring. Do not join rnds or ch 1, just cont to work in rnds as foll:

Rnd 2 Work 2 sc in each sc around—16 sc.

Rnd 3 *Work 1 sc, 2 sc in next sc; rep from * around—24 sc.

Rnd 4 *Work 2 sc, 2 sc in next sc; rep from * around—32 sc.

Rnd 5 *Work 3 sc, 2 sc in next sc; rep from * around—40 sc.

Rnd 6 *Work 4 sc, 2 sc in next sc; rep from * around—48 sc.

Rnd 7 *Work 5 sc, 2 sc in next sc; rep from * around—56 sc.

Rnd 8* Work 6 sc, 2 sc in next sc; rep from * around—64 sc.

Rnd 9 *Work 7 sc, 2 sc in next sc; rep from * around—72 sc.

Rnd 10 *Work 8 sc, 2 sc in next sc; rep from * around—80 sc.

Rnd 11 *Work 9 sc, 2 sc in next sc; rep from * around—88 sc.

Rnd 12 *Work 10 sc, 2 sc in next sc; rep from * around—96 sc.

Rnd 13 Working into back loops only, work even in sc.

Rnds 14-34 Work in both loops, work even in sc.

Beg the brim

Rnd 35 *Work 11 sc, 2 sc in next sc; rep from * around—104 sc.

Rnds 36, 38, 40, 42 and 44 Work even in sc.

Rnd 37 *Work 12 sc, 2 sc in next sc; rep from * around—112 sc.

Rnd 39 *Work 13 sc, 2 sc in next sc; rep from * around—120 sc.

Rnd 41 *Work 14 sc, 2 sc in next sc; rep from * around—128 sc.

Rnd 43 *Work 15 sc, 2 sc in next sc; rep from * around—136 sc.

Rnd 45 Work even in sc.

Rnd 46 Working in back loops only, work even in sc. Fasten off.

FINISHING

Return to the crown edge of rnd 13 and rejoin 1 strand A and B held to to work "welt" from RS. Working through the front loops, work even in sc around rnd 13 to complete welt. Fasten off.

A plain double crochet stitch is segmented by raised ridges to create this perfect-fit hat. Worked from the lower to top edge in this design by Kathy Merrick.

SIZES

Instructions are written for one size.

KNITTED MEASUREMENTS
- Head circumference 22"/56cm
- Depth 7"/17.5cm

MATERIALS
- 1 3½oz/100g skein (each approx 110yd/101m) of Reynolds/JCA *Andean Alpaca Regal* (alpaca/wool) in #606 coral (**5**)
- Size I/9 (5.5mm) crochet hook
  or size to obtain gauge

GAUGE

12 sts and 8 rows/rnds to 4"/10cm over dc pat st using size I/9 (5.5mm) crochet hook. *Take time to check gauge.*

STITCH GLOSSARY

Front post dc (fpdc)

Yarn over hook, insert hook from front to back to front around the stem of the next st, complete dc. Then skip the dc behind the fpdc and cont working.

Dec 1 dc

*Yarn over hook and insert hook into next st, pull up a loop, yo, pull through 2 loops; rep from * in next st, then yo and through all 3 loops on hook.

HAT

Beg at lower edge, ch 66. Join with sl st to first ch being careful not to twist sts of ch.

Rnd 1 Ch 2 (counts as 1 dc), work 1 dc in each ch around, join with sl st to ch-2—66 dc.

Rnd 2 Ch 2, work 4 dc, *fpdc in next st, work 10 dc; rep from *, end fpdc in next st, work 5 dc, join.

Rnds 3-9 Rep rnd 2.

Rnd 10 Ch 2, work 2 dc, dec 1 dc, *fpdc in next dc, dec 1 dc, work 6 dc, dec 1 dc; rep from *, end fpdc in next dc, dec 1 dc, work 3 dc—54 dc.

The lustrous sheen of embroidery floss, coupled with a crayon color box array of colors, gives this hat its very special effects. This striped pillbox hat was designed by Kathy Merrick.

SIZES
Instructions are written for one size.

KNITTED MEASUREMENTS
- Head circumference 21½"/54.5 cm
- Depth 7½"/19 cm

MATERIALS
- 1 18.7yd/8m hank of DMC *Embroidery floss* (cotton) in each of the foll 59 colors:
- Group 1—321, 934, 300, 349, 993, 3860, 824, 436, 894, 733, 500, 924, 350, 3834, 809, 905, 3045, 790, 3851, 936, 915, 3348, 3721, 817, 791, 3829, 902, 834, 498.
- Group 2—666, 898, 522, 826, 165, 777, 356, 720, 550, 3817, 956, 3852, 793, 991, 919, 3045, 912, 434, 3345, 3848, 3819, 3021, 3808, 407, 597, 221, 501, 830, 939, 890.
- Size E/4 (3.5mm) crochet hook *or size to obtain gauge*

GAUGE
- 19 hdc and 32 rows/rnds to 4"/10cm over hdc pat st using double strand of floss and size E/4 (3.5mm) crochet hook. *Take time to check gauge.*

Note Wind the group 1 colors, in the sequence listed, into one ball. Then wind the group 2 colors into a second ball and work entire hat with 1 strand of ball 1 and ball 2 held tog.

STITCH GLOSSARY
Dec 1 hdc
Yo hook and insert hook in next st, yo and draw up a loop, yo and insert hook in next st, yo and draw up a loop, yo and pull through all 5 loops on hook.

HAT
Beg at lower edge with 1 strand of ball 1 and 1 strand of ball 2 held tog, ch 102. Join with sl st to first ch, being careful not to twist ch. Cont to work hat in a spiral, that is do not join or ch on each subsequent rnd.

Rnd 1 Work 1 hdc in each ch around.

Rnds 2-15 Work even in hdc. Piece measures approx 3¾"/9.5 cm from beg.

Rnd 16 Working in back loops only, work even in hdc.

Rnd 17 *Work hdc in each of 7 hdc, dec 1 hdc; rep from *, end beg hdc in each of last 3 hdc—91 hdc.

Rnd 18 Work even in hdc.

Rnd 19 *Dec 1 hdc, work hdc in each of 6 hdc; rep from * end by hdc in each of last 3 hdc—80 hdc.

Rnd 20 Work even in hdc.

Rnd 21 *Work hdc in each of 5 hdc, dec 1 hdc; rep from *, end by hdc in each of last 3 hdc—69 hdc.

Rnd 22 Work even in hdc.

Rnd 23 *Dec 1 hdc, work hdc in each of 4 hdc; rep from *, end by hdc in each of last 3 hdc—58 hdc.

Rnd 24 *Work hdc in each of 3 hdc, dec 1 hdc; rep from *, end by hdc in each of last 3 hdc—47 hdc.

Rnd 25 *Dec 1 hdc, work hdc in each of 2 hdc; rep from *, end by hdc in each of last 3 hdc—36 hdc.

Rnd 26 *Work 1 hdc, dec 1 hdc; rep from * around—24 hdc.

Rnd 27 [Dec 1 hdc] 12 times—12 hdc. Cut yarn leaving a long end. Pull through the rem 12 hdc and draw up tightly and fasten off.

FINISHING

Lower ruffle

To work the lower edge ruffle, rejoin 2 strands of floss in first ch of beg ch. Work 3 hdc in each back loop of the beg ch around. Fasten off.

Top ridge

Locate the (free) front loop on rnd 16, rejoin 2 strands of floss and work 2 sc in each free loop around. Fasten off.

CROCHETED CLOCHE WITH TIE

True blue

A worsted weight basic and a worked-in color tie are the elements that make this cloche a wearable classic. Designed by Mari Lynn Patrick.

SIZES

Instructions are written for size small. Changes for size medium/large are in parentheses. If there is only one number, it applies to both sizes.

KNITTED MEASUREMENTS
■ Head circumference 20 (21½)"/51 (54.5) cm
■ Depth 7½ (7¾)"/19 (19.5) cm

MATERIALS
■ 1 3½oz/100g ball (each approx 245yd/224m) of Brown Sheep Co, Inc. *Nature Spun worsted weight* (wool), each in #117 blue (A) and #119 navy (B) (④)
■ Size J/10 (6mm) crochet hook or size *or size to obtain gauge*

GAUGE

14 sc and 16 rnds to 4"/10cm over sc pat st using size J/10 (6mm) hook. *Take time to check gauge.*

Note When working the sc, ch 1 pat each sc and each ch 1 are referred to as 1 st.

HAT

Beg at top edge with A, ch 4, join with sl st to first ch to form ring.

Rnd 1 Work 6 sc in ring, join with sl st to first st, ch 1.

Rnd 2 Work 2 sc in each st around—12 sts. Join, ch 1.

Rnd 3 [Work 2 sc in next st, 1 sc in next st] 6 times—18 sts. Join, ch 1.

Rnd 4 [Work 2 sc in next st, 1 sc in each of next 2 sts] 6 times—24 sts. Join, ch 1.

Rnd 5 [Work 2 sc in next st, 1 sc in each of next 3 sts] 6 times—30 sts. Join, ch 1.

Rnd 6 [Work 2 sc in next st, 1 sc in each of next 4 sts] 6 times—36 sts. Join, ch 1.

Rnd 7 [Work 2 sc in next st, 1 sc in each of next 5 sts] 6 times—42 sts. Join, ch 1.

Rnd 8 [Work 2 sc in next st, 1 sc in each of next 6 sts] 6 times—48 sts. Join, ch 1.

Rnd 9 [Work 2 sc in next st, 1 sc in each of next 7 sts] 6 times—54 sts. Join, ch 1.

Rnd 10 [Work 2 sc in next st, 1 sc in each of next 8 sts] 6 times—60 sts. Join, ch 1.

Rnd 11 [Work 2 sc in next st, 1 sc in each of next 9 sts] 6 times—66 sts. Join, ch 1.

Rnd 12 [Work 2 sc in next st, 1 sc in each of next 10 sts] 6 times—72 sts. Join, ch 1.

Rnd 13 [Work 2 sc in next st, 1 sc in each of next 11 sts] 6 times—78 sts. Join, ch 1. This is end of crown for size Small.

Size Medium/Large only

Rnd 14 [Work 2 sc in next st, 1 sc in each of next 12 sts] 6 times—84 sts. Join, ch 1. This is end of crown for size Medium/Large.

Rnd 14 (15) *Work 1 sc in back loop of next st, ch 1 and skip 1 sc; rep from *, end join with sl st to first sc.

Rnd 15 (16) Ch 2, skip first sc, *sc in ch-1 space, and skip the sc; rep from *, end sc in last ch-1 space, join with sl st in the first ch-2 space, ch 1.

Rnd 16 (17) Sc in ch-1 space, ch 1 and skip the sc; rep from *, end join with sl st to first sc. Rep rnds 15 and 16 for 6 times more. On last rnd, join with B to first sc.

Rnd 29 (30) With B, ch 2, skip first sc, *sc in ch-1 space, ch 1 and skip the sc; rep from * 14 times more, sc in next ch-1 space then ch 9, sl st in 2nd ch from hook and in each ch (for tie), ch 1 and skip next sc, sc in next ch-1 space, then ch 11, sl st in 2nd ch from hook and in each ch (for tie), complete rnd to end, with A, join to first ch-2 space, ch 1. Cut B.

Rnd 30 (31) With A, *sc in ch-1 space, ch 1 and skip the sc, (sc, ch 1 and sc) in next ch-1 space (for inc), ch 1 and skip the sc, sc in next ch-1 space, ch 1 and skip the sc; rep from *, end ch 1, join with sl st to first sc.

Rnd 31 (32) Rep rnd 15.

Rnd 32 (33) Rep rnd 16.

Rnd 33 (34) Rep rnd 15.

Rnd 34 (35) Sl st in back loops only of each st around. Fasten off. Knot the tie as in photo.

STRIPED CAP

Peek-a-boo

A two-color stripe in single crochet grounds the pattern for this openwork cap, using alternating joinings and chains for the airy effect. This clever design is by Irina Poludnenko.

SIZES
Instructions are written for one size.

KNITTED MEASUREMENTS
- Head circumference 19"/48cm
- Depth 7"/18cm

MATERIALS
- 1 1¾oz/50g ball (each approx 83yd/76m) each of S. Charles Collezione/Tahki•Stacy Charles, Inc. *Merino Cable* (wool) in #111 lt green (A) and #117 gold (B) (4)
- Size G/6 (4.5mm) hook *or size to obtain gauge*

GAUGE
16 sc and 16 rows/rnds to 4"/10cm over sc pat st using size G/6 (4.5mm) crochet hook. *Take time to check gauge.*

Note Stripe pat is formed by 2 rnds A, 2 rnds B. Rep these 4 rnds for stripe pat.

CAP
Beg at crown edge with A, ch 3, join with sl st to first ch to form ring.

Rnd 1 Work 2 sc in each ch around—6 sc. Do not join or ch 1, but cont to work in rnds.

Rnd 2 Work 2 sc in each sc around—12 sc.

Rnd 3 With B, *work 1 sc, 2 sc in next sc; rep from * around—18 sc.

Rnd 4 *Work 2 sc, 2 sc in next sc; rep from * around—24 sc.

Rnd 5 With A, *work 3 sc, 2 sc in next sc; rep from * around—30 sc.

Rnd 6 *Work 4 sc, 2 sc in next sc; rep from * around—36 sc.

Rnd 7 With B, *work 5 sc, 2 sc in next sc; rep from * around—42 sc.

Rnd 8 *Work 6 sc, 2 sc in next sc; rep from * around—48 sc.

Rnd 9 With A, *work 7 sc, 2 sc in next sc; rep from * around—54 sc.

Rnd 10 *Work 8 sc, 2 sc in next sc; rep from * around—60 sc.

Rnd 11 With B, *work 9 sc, 2 sc in next sc; rep from * around—66 sc.

Rnd 12 *Work 10 sc, 2 sc in next sc; rep from * around—72 sc.

Rnd 13 With A, *work 11 sc, 2 sc in next sc; rep from * 4 times more, end by working 12 sc—77 sc.

Rnd 14 With A, work even in sc.

Beg openwork pat

Rnd 15 With B, *work 2 sc, ch 5 and skip 5 sc; rep from * around. There are 11 ch-5 loops.

Rnd 16 With B, *work 2 sc, 1 sc in each of next 5 ch; rep from* around—77 sc.

Rnd 17 and 18 With A, work even in sc.

Rnd 19 With B, *ch 5 and skip 5 sc, work 2 sc; rep from * around.

Rnd 20 With B, *work 1 sc in each of next 5 ch, work 2 sc; rep from * around.

Rnds 21 and 22 With A, work even in sc.

Rnds 23-30 Rep rnds 15–22. Fasten off.

This easy double-crochet mesh pattern is worked up in 15 easy rounds. Designed by Mari Lynn Patrick using one ball of a luxury blend yarn.

SIZES

Instructions are written for one size.

KNITTED MEASUREMENTS

■ Head circumference 19"/48.5cm
■ Depth 7"/18cm

MATERIALS

■ 1 1¾ oz/50g ball (each approx 130 yds/120m) of Berroco, Inc. *Pleasure* (angora/wool/nylon) in #8617 green (4)
■ Size K/10½ (6.5mm) Crochet hook *or size to obtain gauge.*

GAUGE

20 sts and 12 rnds to 4"/10cm over dc mesh pat using size K/10½ (6.5mm). *Take time to check gauge.*

Notes

1 The sts stated in gauge refer to each dc and each ch-1 sp (that is, 2 dc and ch-1 mesh are 3 sts).

2 When instructions say to work into next sc (or sp) at beg of rnd, that means to skip the first st (or space).

CAP

Beg at top edge, ch 5, join with a sl st to first ch to form ring.

Rnd 1 Work 10 sc in ring, join with a sl st to first sc.

Rnd 2 Ch 4 (counts as 1 dc and ch 1), *1 dc in next sc, ch 1; rep from * 8 times more, join with sl st to 3rd ch of ch-4.

Rnd 3 Ch 3 (counts as 1 dc), 1 dc in first ch-1 space, *2 dc in next ch-1 space; rep from * 8 times more, join with sl st to top of ch-3.

Rnd 4 Ch 3 (for first dc of 2-dc group), 1 dc in space after ch 3 of previous rnd, *ch 1, 2 dc in next space, ch 1, skip 2 dc, 2 dc in space after these 2 dc, ch 1, skip 1 dc, 2 dc in next dc (for 2-sc group inc); rep from * 3 times more, end ch 1, 2 dc in next space, ch 1, skip 2 dc, 2 dc in last space, ch 1, join with sl st to top of ch-3—15 2-dc groups.

Rnd 5 Ch 3, skip ch-3 and dc, *2 dc in next ch-1 space, ch 1; rep from * 14 times more, end sl st to top of ch-3.

Rnd 6 Ch 3, 2 dc in space after ch-3 of previous rnd, *[ch 1, 2 dc in next ch-1 space] twice, ch 1, skip 1 dc, 2 dc in 2nd dc of 2-dc group, ch 1, 2 dc in next ch-1 space; rep from * 3 times more, end [ch 1, 2 dc in next ch-1 space] 3 times, ch 1, join to top of ch-3-21 groups.

Rnd 7 Ch 3, 2 dc in space after ch-3 of

previous rnd, [ch 1, 2 dc in next ch-1 space] 20 times, ch 1, join with sl st to top of ch-3.

Rnd 8 Ch 3, skip first 2 dc group, [2 dc in next ch-1 space, ch-1] 21 times, join to top of ch-3.

Rnds 9-13 Rep rnd 8.

Rnd 14 Ch 1, *sc in each of next 2 dc, 1 sc in next ch-1 space; rep from * to end, join with sl st to first sc.

Rnd 15 Ch 2, 1 hdc in back lps only of each sc around. Join and fasten off.

QUILTED EFFECT HAT
Patchwork perfect

Crocheted motifs are worked in hexagonal and pentagonal shapes to make up this quilted effect hat, which is trimmed at the edge in backwards single crochet. Designed by Anna Mishka.

SIZES

Instructions are written for one size.

KNITTED MEASUREMENTS

- Head circumference 21"/53cm
- Depth 7¾"/19.5cm

MATERIALS

- 1 4oz/113g skein (each approx 215yd/198m) of Brown Sheep Yarn Co. *Cotton Fleece* (cotton/wool) each in #660 blush (A), #230 victorian pink (B), #930 candy apple (C) and #140 grey dawn (D) (4)
- Size D/4 (3mm) crochet hook *or size to obtain gauge*

GAUGE

One motif is 2¾"/7cm across between the points. *Take time to check gauge.*

HAT

MOTIF I

(Make 4)

Row I (RS)

With C, ch 3, join with sl st to first ch to form ring.

Rnd I Ch 1, work 6 sc in ring, join with sl st to first st on this and all foll rnds. Cut C.

Rnd 2 Join A with sl st in any sc, ch 2 (yo and draw up a loop) twice in same sc, yo and draw through all loops on hook and ch 1 for beg cluster, ch 2 (yo and draw up a loop) 3 times in same sc as beg cluster, yo and through all loops on hook and ch 1 (for cluster), *(work cluster, ch 2, cluster) in next sc; rep from * 4 times more, join to top of first cluster. Cut A.

Rnd 3 Join D with sl st in any ch-2 space, ch 1 (1 sc, ch 2, 1 sc) in same space as sl st, * 3 sc between next 2 clusters, (1 sc, ch 2, 1 sc) in next ch-2 space; rep from* 4 times more, end 3 sc between next 2 clusters, join. Cut D.

Rnd 4 Join A with sl st in any ch-2 space, ch 1, (1 sc, ch 2, 1 sc) in same space as sl st, * 1 sc in each of next 5 sc, (1 sc, ch 2, 1 sc) in next ch-2 space; rep from * 4 times more, end 1 sc in each of last 5 sc. Join and fasten off.

MOTIF 2

(Make 4)

Work as for motif 1, only work rnd 1 with B, rnd 2 with D, rnd 3 with C and rnd 4 with D.

MOTIF 3

(Make 5)

With A, ch 3, join with sl st to form ring.

Rnd 1 Ch 2, work 12 hdc in ring, join to first hdc. Cut A.

Rnd 2 Join C with sl st to any hdc, ch 1, 2 sc in same st with sl st, 2 sc in each of next 11 hdc, join D with sl st to first sc—24 sc. Cut C.

Rnd 3 Join D with sl st in any sc, ch 2, 2 hdc in same st with sl st, *ch 1, skip 1 sc, 2 hdc in next sc, ch 2, skip 1 sc, 2 hdc in next sc; rep from * 4 times more, ch 1, skip next sc, 2 hdc in 1 sc, ch 2, join to first hdc. Cut D.

Rnd 4 Join B with sl st in any ch-2 space, ch 1 (1 sc, ch 2, 1 sc), in same space as sl st, *1 sc in each of next 2 hdc, 1 sc in next ch-1 space, 1 sc in each of next 2 hdc, (1 sc, ch 2, 1 sc) in next ch-2 space; rep from * 4 times more, end 1 sc in each of next 2 hdc, 1 sc in next ch-1 space, 1 sc in each of next 2 hdc. Join and fasten off.

MOTIF 4

(Make 4)

Work as for motif 3, only work rnd 1 with B, rnd 2 with D, rnd 3 with A and rnd 4 with B.

MOTIF 5

(Make 2)

With C, ch 3, join with sl st to form ring.

Rnd 1 Ch 1, work 5 sc in ring, join and fasten off C.

Rnd 2 Join A with sl st in any sc, ch 2, (yo and draw up a loop) twice in same sc, yo and draw through all loops on hook and ch 1 (for beg cluster), ch 2, (yo and draw up a loop) 3 times in same sc as beg cluster, yo and through all loops on hook and ch 1 (for cluster), *(work cluster, ch 2, cluster) in next sc; rep from * 3 times more, join. Cut A.

Rnd 3 Join D with sl st in any ch-2 space, ch 1 (1 sc, ch 2, 1 sc) in same space, *3 sc between next 2 clusters, (1 sc, ch 2, 1 sc) in next ch-2 space; rep from * 3 times more, end 3 sc between next 2 clusters, join. Cut D.

Rnd 4 Join A with sl st in any ch-2 space, ch 1, (1 sc, ch 2, 1 sc) in same space, *1 sc in each of next 5 sc, (1 sc, ch 2, 1 sc) in next ch-2 space; rep from * 3 times more, end 1 sc in each of last 5 sc. Join and fasten off.

MOTIF 6

(Make 2)

Work as for motif 5, only work rnd 1 with B, rnd 2 with D, rnd 3 with C and rnd 4 with D.

MOTIF 7

(Make 2)

With A, ch 3, join with sl st to form ring.

Rnd 1 Ch 2, work 10 hdc in ring, join to first hdc. Cut A.

Rnd 2 Join C with sl st to any hdc, ch 1, 2 sc in same st with sl st, 2 sc in each of next 9 hdc, join D with sl st to first sc—20 sc. Cut C.

Rnd 3 Join D with sl st in any sc, ch 2, 2 hdc in same st with sl st, *ch 1, skip 1 sc, 2 hdc in next sc, ch 2, skip 1 sc, 2 hdc in next sc; rep from * 3 times more, ch 1, skip next sc, 2 hdc in next sc, ch 2, join to first hdc. Cut D.

Rnd 4 Join B with sl st in any ch-2 space, ch 1, (1 sc, ch 2, 1 sc) in same space as sl st, *1 sc in each of next 2 hdc, 1 sc in next ch-1 space, 1 sc in each of next 2 hdc, (1 sc, ch 2, 1 sc) in next ch-2 space; rep from * 3 times more, end 1 sc in each of next 2 hdc, 1 sc in next ch-1 space, 1 sc in each of next 2 hdc. Join and fasten off.

MOTIF 8

(Make 2)

Work as for motif 7, only work rnd 1 with B, rnd 2 with D, rnd 3 with A and rnd 4 with B.

JOINING MOTIFS

Hat is composed of 3 sets of joined strips (with 8 motifs in each strip) and a center top motif. Use D to sl st the motifs tog on WS along one edge only.

First strip

For the lower edge strip (alternate motifs 1 or 2 with motifs 3 or 4) 4 times.

Second strip

For the center strip, work as for first strip, alternating colors as before.

Third strip

For the top (crown strip), alternate motifs 5, 6, 7 and 8 randomly foll photo. Be sure to have 2 sides of each pentagon free on one side of the strip and one side of each pentagon free on opposite side of strip.

TOP MOTIF

Use rem motif 3 for top of hat and join all strips tog to form hat.

LOWER EDGE

Rnd 1 Join B with sl st in any ch-2 space, *1 sc in each of next 2 sc, 1 hdc in each of next 2 sc, 1 dc in each of next 2 sc, yo hook twice and draw up a loop in next sc, (yo and through 2 loops) twice, yo hook twice and draw up a loop in next ch-2 space, (yo and through 2 loops) twice, yo hook twice and draw up a loop in next ch-2 space of next motif, (yo and through 2 loops) twice, yo hook twice, and draw up a loop in next sc, (yo and draw through 2 loops) twice, yo and draw through all 5 loops—Tr4tog made, 1 dc in each of next 2 sc, 1 hdc in each of next 2 sc, 1 sc in each of next 2 sc, sl st in ch-2 space; rep from * around join to first sc. Cut B.

Rnd 2 Join D with sl st in last sl st, ch 1, 1 sl in same space as sl st, *ch 1, skip 1 st, 1 sc in next st; rep from * to last st, ch 1, skip last st, join to to first sc. Cut D.

Rnd 3 Join A in any sc, ch 1, 1 sc in first sc, * 1 sc in next st located 1 row below next ch-1 space, 1 sc in next sc; rep from * to last ch-1 space, 1 sc in next st 1 row below as before, join with sl st to first sc.

Rnd 4 With A, working from left to right, work 1 reverse sc in each sc around. Fasten off.

■■□□

Multiple colors play out with white—all in one yarn—to give this tall crowned hat a modern edge. Bobble trim above the brim accents this flirty creation by Kathy Merrick.

SIZES

Instructions are written for one size.

KNITTED MEASUREMENTS

■ Head circumference 21"/53 cm
■ Depth (including brim) 10"/25.5 cm

MATERIALS

■ 2 3½oz/100g skeins (each approx 100yd/92m) of Naturwolle/Muench Yarns *Black Forest Multi* (wool) in #3 kunterbunt (**4**)
■ Size I/9 (5.5mm) crochet hook *or size to obtain gauge*

GAUGE

13 sc and 16 rows/rnds to 4"/10cm over sc pat using size I/9 (5.5mm) crochet hook. *Take time to check gauge.*

STITCH GLOSSARY

Dec 1 sc

Insert hook in next st, yo and draw up a loop, insert hook in next st, yo and draw up a loop, yo and through all 3 loops on hook.

Bobble

Work 4 dc all into one st, remove hook, insert from front of work into first dc, insert hook through loop of last dc, pull loop through first dc.

CLOCHE

Beg at crown edge, ch 4, join with sl st to form ring.

Rnd 1 Work 8 sc in ring. Do not join or ch 1 on this or foll rnds, work rnds in a spiral.

Rnd 2 Work 2 sc in each sc around— 16 sc.

Rnd 3 *Work 1 sc, 2 sc in next sc; rep from * around—24 sc.

Rnd 4 *Work 2 sc, 2 sc in next sc; rep from * around—32 sc.

Rnd 5 *Work 3 sc, 2 sc in next sc; rep from * around—40 sc.

Rnd 6 *Work 4 sc, 2 sc in next sc; rep from * around—48 sc.

Rnd 7 *Work 5 sc, 2 sc in next sc; rep from * around—56 sc.

Rnd 8 *Work 6 sc, 2 sc in next sc; rep from * around—64 sc.

Rnds 9-18 Work even in sc.

Rnd 19 *Work bobble, 1 sc in each of next 3 sc, rep from * around.

Rnd 20 Work even in sc.

Rnd 21 *Work 3 sc, work bobble in next sc; rep from * around.

Rnds 22 and 23 Work even in sc.

Rnd 24 *Work 7 sc, 2 sc in next sc; rep

from * around—72 sc.

Rnds 25, 27, 29, 31 and 33 Work even in sc.

Rnd 26 *Work 8 sc, 2 sc in next sc; rep from * around—80 sc.

Rnd 28 *Work 9 sc, 2 sc in next sc; rep from * around—88 sc.

Rnd 30 *Work 10 sc, 2 sc in next sc; rep from * around—96 sc.

Rnd 32 *Work 11 sc, 2 sc in next sc; rep from * around—104 sc.

Rnd 34 *Work 12 sc, 2 sc in next sc; rep from * around—112 sc.

Rnd 35 Work even in sc. Fasten off.

STRIPED HELMET
Andean treasure

■◼▭▭

Two alternating balls of length-dyed yarn yield a dazzling effect of color stripes. The earflap stripe is worked organically into the circular head pattern. After working in single crochet, turn it inside-out and trim it with tiny fringes. Designed by Irina Poludnenko.

SIZES

Instructions are written for one size.

KNITTED MEASUREMENTS

■ Head circumference 20"/51cm
■ Depth 8"/20.5cm

MATERIALS

■ 1 1¾oz/50g ball (each approx 110yd/101m) each of Noro/Knitting Fever Yarns *Kureyon* (wool) in #88 (A) and #95 (B) (4)
■ Size H/8 (5mm) crochet hook *or size to obtain gauge*

GAUGE

14 sc and 16 rows/rnds to 4"/10 cm over sc pat st using size H/8 (5mm) crochet hook. *Take time to check gauge.*

Notes

1 Stripe pattern is formed by working 3 rnds from ball A, then 3 rnds from ball B.
2 Hat is turned inside out when completed.

HELMET

Beg at top edge with A, ch 4, join with sl st to first ch to form ring. Place yarn marker to mark beg of rnd. Do not join, but work hat in a spiral.

Rnd 1 (A) Work 2 sc in each ch around—8 sc.

Rnd 2 (A) Work 2 sc in each sc around—16 sc.

Rnd 3 (A) *Work 1 sc, 2 sc in next sc; rep from * around—24 sc.

Rnd 4 (B) *Work 2 sc, 2 sc in next sc; rep from * around—32 sc.

Rnd 5 (B) *Work 3 sc, 2 sc in next sc; rep from * around—40 sc.

Rnd 6 (B) *Work 4 sc, 2 sc in next sc; rep from * around—48 sc.

Rnd 7 (A) *Work 5 sc, 2 sc in next sc; rep from * around—56 sc.

Rnd 8 (A) *Work 6 sc, 2 sc in next sc; rep from * around—64 sc.

Working 1 more rnd with A, then 3 rnds B, 3 rnds A, work even on 64 sc for 8 rnds. Stripe pat should cont to end of helmet.

EARFLAPS

Next rnd Work 13 sc, ch 7, work 1 sc in each of the 7 ch, work 38 sc, ch 7, work 1 sc in each of the 7 ch, work 13 sc—78 sts. Cont to work helmet with earflaps as foll:

Rnd 1 Work 12 sc, *skip next sc (for dec), work 6 sc, work 3 sc in next sc, work 3 sc in next sc (earflap corner), work 6 sc, skip next sc (for dec)*, work 22 sc; rep between *'s for 2nd earflap, work rem 12 sc—82 sts.

Rnd 2 Work 11 sc, *skip next st, work 7 sc, 3 sc in next sc, work 2 sc, 3 sc in next sc (corner), work 7 sc, skip next st*, work 20 sc; rep between *'s once, work 11 sc— 86 sts.

Rnd 3 Work 10 sc, *skip next st, work 7 sc, 3 sc in next sc, work 6 sc, 3 sc in next sc, work 7 sc, skip next st*, work 18 sc; rep between *'s once work 10 sc— 90 sts.

Rnd 4 Work 9 sc, *skip next st, work 7 sc, 3 sc in next sc, work 10 sc, 3 sc in next sc, work 7 sc, skip next st*; work 16 sc; rep between *'s once, work 9 sc— 94 sts.

Rnd 5 Work 8 sc, *skip next st, work 7 sc, 3 sc in next sc, work 14 sc, 3 sc in next sc, work 7 sc, skip next st*, work 14 sc; rep between *'s once, work 8 sc—98 sts.

Rnd 6 Work 7 sc, * skip next st, work 7 sc, 3 sc in next sc, work 18 sc, 3 sc in next sc, work 7 sc, skip next st*, work 12 sc; rep between *'s once, work 7 sc—102 sts.

Rnd 7 Work 7 sc, *skip next st, work 7 sc, 2 sc in next sc, work 18 sc, 2 sc in next sc; work 7 sc, skip next st*, work 16 sc; rep between *'s once, work 7 sc—102 sts.

Rnds 8-13 Rep rnd 7. Fasten off.

FINISHING

Cut 3 strands of yarn each approx 2"/5cm long. Make 9 fringes on each earflap (as in photo) and trim.

■■□□

Moody dark tweed yarns combine with black in this cap reminiscent of a Turkish kilim rug pattern. The crown is topped with a simple flower and the final round of shells is trimmed with little picots in this cap designed by Sasha Kagan.

SIZES

Instructions are written for one size.

KNITTED MEASUREMENTS
■ Head circumference 20"/51 cm
■ Depth 7½"/19 cm

MATERIALS
■ 1 .88oz/25g hank (each approx 120yd/110m) of Rowan Yarns *Yorkshire Tweed 4-Ply* (wool) each in #283 black (A), #273 rust (B), #274 red (C) and #269 lt. purple (D) (4)
■ Size C/2 (2.75mm) crochet hook *or size to obtain gauge*

GAUGE

21 sc and 25 rows/rnds to 4"/10cm over sc pat st using size C/2 (2.75mm) crochet hook. *Take time to check gauge.*

CAP

Beg at top edge with A, ch 4, join with sl st to first ch to form ring.

Rnd I Ch 1, work 8 sc in ring, join with sl st to first sc.

Rnd 2 Ch 1, work 2 sc in each sc around, join—16 sc.

Rnd 3 Ch 1, work even in sc, join.

Rnd 4 Ch 1, *work 1 sc in next sc, 2 sc in next sc; rep from * around, join—24 sc.

Rnd 5 Ch 1, work even in sc, join.

Rnd 6 Ch 1, *work 1 sc in each of next 2 sc, 2 sc in next sc; rep from * around, join—32 sc.

Rnd 7 Ch 1, work even in sc, join.

Rnd 8 Ch 1, *work 1 sc in each of next 3 sc, 2 sc in next sc; rep from * around, join—40 sc.

Rnd 9 With B, ch 1, work even in sc, join.

Rnd 10 With B, ch 1, working in back loops only, *work 1 sc in each of next 4 sc, 2 sc in next sc; rep from * around, join—48 sc.

Rnd 11 With A, ch 1, work even in sc, join.

Rnd 12 With A, ch 1, *work 1 sc in each of next 5 sc, 2 sc in next sc; rep from * around, join—56 sc.

Rnd 13 With C, ch 1, work even in sc, join.

Rnd 14 With C, ch 1, working in back loops only, *work 1 sc in each of next 6 sc, 2 sc in next sc; rep from * around, join—64 sc.

Rnd 15 With A, ch 1, work even in sc, join.

Rnd 16 With D, ch 1, working in back loops only, *work 1 sc in each of next 7

51

sc, 2 sc in next sc; rep from * around, join—72 sc.

Rnd 17 With D, ch 1, working in back loops only, work even in sc, join.

Rnd 18 With A, ch 1, working in back loops only, *work 1 sc in each of next 8 sc, 2 sc in next sc; rep from * around, join—80 sc.

Rnd 19 With C, ch 1, work even in sc, join.

Rnd 20 With C, ch 1, working in back loops only, *work 1 sc in each of next 9 sc, 2 sc in next sc; rep from * around, join—88 sc.

Rnd 21 With A, ch 1, working in back loops only, work even in sc, join.

Rnd 22 With A, ch 1, *work 1 sc in each of next 10 sc, 2 sc in next sc; rep from * around, join—96 sc.

Rnd 23 With B, ch 1, work even in sc, join.

Rnd 24 With B, ch 1, working in back loops only, *work 1 sc in each of next 11 sc, 2 sc in next sc; rep from * around, join—104 sc.

Rnd 25 With A, ch 1, working in back loops only, work even in sc, join.

Rnd 26 With A, ch 1, work even in sc, join.

Beg shell pattern

Rnd 27 With A, ch 3, work 4 sc in next sc, *skip 2 sc, sl st in next sc, skip 2 sc, 5 dc in next sc (for shell); rep from *, end skip 2 sc, sl st in next sc, fasten off A.

Rnd 28 Join B in top of last sl st, ch 3, work 4 dc in this sl st, *work 1 sl st in 3rd dc of next shell, work shell in next sl st; rep from *, end work 1 sl st in 3rd dc of last shell. Fasten off B.

Rnds 29, 31, 33, 35 and 37 With A, rep rnd 28.

Rnd 30 With C, rep rnd 28

Rnd 32 With D, rep rnd 28.

Rnd 34 With C, rep rnd 28.

Rnd 36 With B, rep rnd 28.

Picot rnd 38 With A, *in top of shell

work ch 3, sl st in same space as sl st, sl st in next 5 sts; rep from * around, join and fasten off.

FLOWER

With D, ch 3, join with sl st to first ch to form ring.

Rnd 1 Work 9 sc in ring, join with sl st to first sc.

Rnd 2 Ch 1, work 2 sc in each sc around, join—18 sc.

Rnd 3 *Ch 5, skip 2 sc, sl st in next sc; rep from * around—6 loops. Join and fasten off D.

Rnd 4 Join C in one ch-5 loop, *in ch-5 loop, work 1 sl st, 1 sc, 5 dc, 1 sc and 1 sl st; rep from * 5 times more. Fasten off. Sew flower to top of cap.

BEEHIVE HAT

A taste of honey

■■□□

Cluster treble bobbles trim the double crochet base of this beehive-inspired hat. Designed in a luxurious silk and mohair blend yarn by Gitta Schrade.

STITCH GLOSSARY

Bobble st

*Yo hook twice (as for tr st), insert hook from front to back to front around base of next dc, [yo hook and through 2 loops] twice; then with rem loops on hook, rep from * 4 times more, then draw through all 5 loops on hook and tighten for closure.

HAT

Beg at top edge, ch 5, join with sl st to first ch to form ring.

Rnd 1 Ch 3 (counts as 1 dc), work 12 dc in ring, join with sl st to top of ch-3.

Rnd 2 Ch 3, [2 dc in next dc] 12 times, join—25 dc.

Rnd 3 Ch 3, [2 dc in next dc, 1 dc in next dc] 12 times, join—37 dc.

Rnd 4 Ch 3, [2 dc in next dc, 1 dc in each of next 2 dc] 12 times, join—49 dc.

Rnd 5 Ch 3, [2 dc in next dc, 1 dc in each of next 3 dc] 12 times, join—61 dc.

Rnd 6 Ch 3, [2 dc in next dc, 1 dc in each of next 5 dc] 10 times, join—71 dc.

Rnd 7 Ch 3, 1 dc in each of next 7 dc, [2 dc in next dc, 1 dc in each of next 8 dc] 7 times, join—78 dc.

Rnd 8 Ch 3, [2 dc in next dc, 1 dc in each of next 10 dc] 7 times, join—85 dc.

Rnds 9 and 10 Ch 3, work even in dc.

Rnd 11 Ch 3, [1 dc in each of next 5 dc, bobble st around next dc] 14 times, join.

Rnd 12 Ch 3, work even in dc.

Rnd 13 Ch 3, [1 dc in each of next 2 dc, bobble st around next dc, 1 dc in each of next 3 dc] 14 times, join.

Rnd 14 Ch 3, work even in dc.

Rep rnds 11–14 once more. Rep rnd 11 once. Fasten off.

GRANNY SQUARE CAP

Mosaic magic

Miniature squares are worked in a variety of colors and then finished in strips for the granny square sections of this cap. Multicolor striping finishes the effect in this design by Gitta Schrade.

SIZES
Instructions are written for one size.

KNITTED MEASUREMENTS
- Head circumference 18"/45.5 cm
- Depth 7¼"/18.5 cm

MATERIALS
- 1 1¾oz/50g ball (each approx 135yd/142m) of Filatura di Crosa/Tahki•Stacy Charles, Inc. *Zara* (wool) each in #1700 purple (A), #1723 pink (B), #1404 black (C), #1461 wine (D) and #1666 fuchsia (E) ④
- Size E/4 (3.5mm) crochet hook *or size to obtain gauge*

GAUGE
17 dc and 12 dc rows/rnds to 4"/10cm over dc pat st using size E/4 (3.5mm) crochet hook. *Take time to check gauge.*

CAP
Beg at top edge with A, ch 5, join with sl st to first ch to form ring.

Rnd 1 With A, ch 3 (counts as 1 dc on this and all foll rnds), work 12 dc in ring, join with sl st to top of beg chain on this and all foll rnds.

Rnd 2 With B, ch 3, [work 2 dc in next dc] 12 times, join—25 dc.

Rnd 3 With C, ch 2, [2 sc in next dc, 1 sc in next dc] 12 times, join—37 sc.

Rnd 4 With D, ch 3, [2 dc in next sc, 1 dc in each of next 2 sc] 12 times, join—49 dc.

Rnd 5 With E, ch 3, [2 dc in next dc, 1 dc in each of next 3 dc] 12 times, join—61 dc.

Rnd 6 With C, ch 2, [2 sc in next dc, 1 sc in each of next 5 dc] 10 times, join—71 sc.

Rnd 7 With A, ch 3, 1 dc in each of next 7 sc, [2 dc in next sc, 1 dc in each of next 8 sc] 7 times, join—78 dc.

Rnd 8 With B, ch 3, [2 dc in next dc, 1 dc in each of next 10 dc] 7 times, join—85 dc. Lay work aside.

GRANNY SQUARE
- Make six square 1 squares in the foll color sequence: D, B, C.
- Make six square 2 squares in the foll color sequence: E, A, C.
- Make six square 3 squares in the foll color sequence: A, E, D.
- Make six square 4 squares in the foll

color sequence: B, C, D.

With D (E, A or B), ch 5, join with sl st to first ch to form ring.

Rnd 1 Ch 3 (counts as 1 sc and ch 2), work 1 sc, ch 2, (2 sc, ch 2) 3 times in ring, join with sl st to 2nd ch of ch-3.

Rnd 2 Join next color in any ch-2 loop, ch 3, work 1 sc in each of next 2 sc, 1 sc in ch-2 loop, ch 2, [1 sc in ch-2 loop, 1 sc in each of next 2 sc, 1 sc in ch-2 loop, ch 2] 3 times, join.

Rnd 3 Join next color in any ch-2 loop, ch 3, work 1 sc in each of next 4 sc, 1 sc in ch-2 loop, ch 2, [1 sc in ch-2 loop, 1 sc in each of next 4 sc, 1 sc in ch-2 loop, ch 2] 3 times, join and fasten off. For strip 1, join (square 1 to square 2) 6 times by sl st tog on WS. For Strip 2, join (square 3 to square 4) 6 times by sl st tog on WS.

With WS facing and C, sl st strips 1 to the crown of the hat on hold.

SECOND STRIPE SECTION

Rnd 1 With C, ch 2, work 84 sc evenly around lower edge of strip 1, join—85 sc.

Rnd 2 With B, ch 3, work 84 dc around, join.

Rnd 3 With A, rep rnd 2.

Rnd 4 With E, rep rnd 2.

Rnd 5 With C, ch 2, work even in sc around, join and lay work aside. From WS, sl st strip 2 to the last rnd of the 2nd stripe section.

Next rnd With B, ch 3, work 84 dc around, join—85 dc.

Next rnd With A, ch 3, work even in dc, join.

Last rnd With E, ch 2, work even in sc. Join and fasten off.

MOHAIR STRIPE CAP

Lavender confection

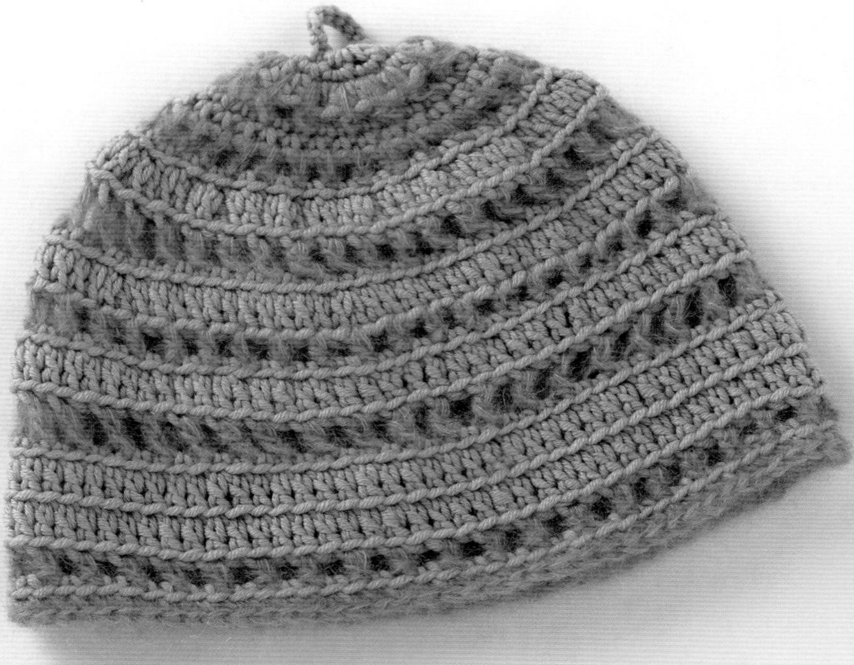

Smooth wool striping in a creamy shade of lavender is set off by openwork rows of lace mohair in a coordinating heavenly hue of purple. Designed with a self-hanging loop by Mari Lynn Patrick.

SIZES

Instructions are written for one size.

KNITTED MEASUREMENTS

- Head circumference 20"/51cm
- Depth 7"/18cm

MATERIALS

- 1 1¾oz/50g ball (each approx 98yd/90m Karabella Yarns *Aurora 8 ply* (wool) in #9 lavender (A) (4)
- 1 1¾oz/50g ball (each approx 540yd/500m) of Karabella Yarns *Lace Mohair* (mohair/wool/polyamide) in #32020 purple (B) (4)
- Size G/7 (4.5mm) crochet hook *or size to obtain gauge*

GAUGE

4 dc and 2 dc rnds to 4"/10cm over sc pat using size G/7 (4.5mm) hook and A. *Take time to check gauge.*

Notes

1 Each sc, dc, hdc or ch 1 are all referred to as 1 st when starting the st counts.

2 Work with 3 strands of B on each rnd worked with B. To get 3 strands from one ball, wind off a small double strand ball from center and outside of ball. Then join this ball to 1 strand ball.

CAP

Beg at top edge with A, leaving a long end (for loop to be worked later), ch 4, join with sl st to first ch to form ring.

Rnd 1 Work 8 sc in ring, join with sl st to first sc, ch 1.

Rnd 2 Work 2 sc in each sc around—16 sts. Join with sl st to first st.

Rnd 3 Ch 2, work 2 hdc in each sc around—32 sts. With 3 strands B, join to first st.

Rnd 4 With 3 strands B, ch 3, then yo hook and working into rnd 2 (and covering the hdc on rnd 3), work 1 dc in next sc of rnd 2, *ch 1 and skip next hdc, work 1 dc in next sc of rnd 2; rep from * 14 times more, end sl st with A to top of ch-3. There are 16 spike dc sts and 16 ch-1 spaces.

Rnd 5 With A, ch 1, work 1 sc in each dc and each ch-1 around—32 sts.

Rnd 6 With A, ch 1, *1 sc and ch 1 in next sc; rep from * 31 times more—64 sts. With 3 strands B, join to first st.

Rnd 7 With 3 strands B, ch 2, skip first sc, *1 hdc in ch-1 space, ch 1 and skip 1 sc; rep from *, end join with A to ch 2.

Rnd 8 With A, ch 2, *skip 1 hdc, 1 sc in ch-1 space, ch 1; rep from *, end sl st in ch-2 space.

Rnd 9 With A, ch 3, then working in back loops only, *work 1 dc in each of next 3 sts, 2 dc in next st; rep from *, end draw 3 strands B through last 2 loops, join to ch-3.

Rnd 10 With 3 strands B, ch 4, then working in back loops only, skip first dc, *dc in next dc, ch 1, skip 1 dc; rep from *, end sl st with A in 3rd ch of ch 4.

Rnd 11 With A, ch 1, work 1 sc in each dc and 1 sc in each ch-1 space around—76 sc. Join with sl st to first sc.

Rnd 12 With A, ch 3, working in back loops only, 1 dc in each of next 4 sc, *2 dc in next sc, 1 dc in each of next 11 sc; rep from *, end 2 dc in next sc, 1 dc in each of last 10 sc—80 dc. Join 3 strands B with sl st to ch-3.

Rnd 13 With 3 strands B, ch 2, *hdc in next dc, ch 1 and skip 1 dc; rep from *end hdc in last dc, ch 1, with A, join with sl st to ch-2.

Rnd 14 With A, ch 2, skip first hdc, *1 sc in ch-1 space, ch 1 and skip 1 hdc; rep from *, end 1 sc in ch-1 space, join to first sc.

Rnd 15 Ch 3, working in back loops only, work 1 dc in each sc and each ch-1 space around, join with 3 strands B to first sc.

Rnd 16 Rep rnd 10.

Rnd 17 Rep rnd 11.

Rnd 18 With A, ch 3, working into back loops only, work 1 dc in each sc around. Join.

Rnd 19 With A, ch 3, working into back loops only, work 1 dc in each dc around, join 3 strands B with sl st to top of ch-3.

Rnd 20 Work 3 strands B, ch 2, working in back loops only, work 1 hdc in first dc, *ch 1 and skip 1 dc, 1 hdc in next dc; rep from *, end ch 1, skip 1 dc, join A with sl st to ch 2.

Rnd 21 With A, ch 2, skip first hdc, *sc in ch-1 space, ch 1 and skip 1 hdc; rep from * around. With 3 strands B, join with sl st to ch 2. Cut A.

Rnd 22 With 3 strands B, ch 1 working into back loops only, sc in each sc and ch-1 space around. Join to first sc. Fasten off.

FINISHING

Block the cap on a head form using a damp cloth. Leave cap to dry. Return to the long strand in A at the top and pull to RS. Ch 8, join to opposite side of ring. Sl st in each ch and join to top. Fasten off and secure.

Semi-attached circles trim the lower edge of this cozy alpaca hat worked up in easy double crochet. Cap is designed by Doris Chan.

SIZES

Instructions are written for one size.

KNITTED MEASUREMENTS

- Head circumference 21"/53 cm
- Depth 7½"/19 cm

MATERIALS

- 2 2oz/60g hanks (each approx 120yd/110m) of Blue Sky Alpaca *Alpaca Sportweight* (alpaca) in #23 red (A) (**4**)
- 1 hank in #73 gold (B)
- Size G/6 (4.5mm) crochet hook or *size to obtain gauge*

GAUGES

- 16 dc and 10 rows/rnds to 4"/10cm over dc pat st using size G/6 (4.5mm) crochet hook.
- One circle motif is 1½"/4cm wide.
Take time to check gauges.

STITCH GLOSSARY

Puff st (or hdc2tog)

Working all into 1 space, [yo, insert hook, yo and draw up a loop] twice, yo and draw through all 5 loops on hook.

Note Cap is worked back and forth in joined rnds, 1 rnd from RS and 1 rnd from WS.

With A, ch 4, sl st to first ch to form ring.

Rnd 1 (RS) Ch 3 (counts as 1 dc), work 11 dc in ring, sl st in top of beg ch, turn—12 dc.

Rnd 2 (WS) Ch 3, dc in same st as joining, 2 dc in each of next 11 dc, join with sl st to top of beg ch on this and all rnds, turn—24 dc.

Rnd 3 Ch 3, [2 dc in next dc, dc in next dc] 11 times, 2 dc in last dc, join and turn—36 dc.

Rnd 4 Ch 3, dc in next dc, [2 dc in next dc, dc in each of next 2 dc] 11 times, 2 dc in last dc, join and turn—48 dc.

Rnd 5 Ch 3, dc in each of next 2 dc, [2 dc in next dc, dc in each of next 3 dc] 11 times, 2 dc in last dc, join and turn—60 dc.

Rnd 6 Ch 3, dc in each of next 3 dc, [2 dc in next dc, dc in each of next 4 dc] 11 times, 2 dc in last dc, join and turn—72 dc.

Rnd 7 Ch 3, dc in each of next 4 dc, [2 dc in next dc, dc in each of next 5 dc] 11 times, 2 dc in last dc, join and turn—84 dc.

Rnds 8-16 Ch 3, work 1 dc in each dc around, join and turn.

Rnd 17 (RS) Ch 1, sc in same st as joining, [ch 1, skip next dc, sc in each of next 3 dc, ch 1, skip next dc, sc in each of next 2 dc] 12 times, only on the last rep, omit last sc and join with sl st to first sc and fasten off. There are 24 ch-spaces. Place yarn marker to indicate the last ch-1 space worked on rnd.

There are 12 motifs first worked separately for rnd 1 with B, then joined to cap lower edge and to each circle on the 2nd rnd while working as foll:

FIRST MOTIF

Center

With B, ch 3, join with sl st to first ch to form ring.

Rnd 1 Ch 2, 1 hdc in ring (counts as beg puff st), [ch 1, work 1 puff st] 5 times into ring, ch 1, join with sl st to beg puff st, fasten off. There are 6 puff sts and 6 ch-spaces. Make 12 rnd 1 puffs in B (for 12 centers).

MOTIF 1

Joining rnd 2 Join A with sl st in one ch-1 space of center (ch 1, hdc, ch 1, puff st) in same ch-space, [ch 1, puff st] twice in each of the next 3 ch-spaces, ch 1, sl st in marked ch-space of the cap, *[puff st, ch 1] twice in next ch-space of center, skip next 2 sc on cap, sl st in next ch-space of cap, [puff st, ch 1] twice in last ch-space of center, sl st to top of beg puff st. Fasten off.

MOTIFS 2-11

Joining rnd 2 Join A with sl st in any ch-1 space of center, (ch 1, hdc, ch 1, puff st) in same ch-space, [ch 1, puff st] twice in each of next 2 ch-spaces, ch 1, sl st in last ch-space of the previous joined motif, [puff st, ch 1] twice in next ch-space of center, skip next 3 sc of cap, sl st in next ch-space of cap, then cont from * of first motif rnd 2 to end.

MOTIF 12

Joining rnd 2 Work as for motif 11, only omit the last sl st in corresponding ch-space of motif 1 and instead sl st in top of beg puff st. Fasten off.

Color-dyed ribbon yarn in shades of autumn leaves is crocheted in this cloche style with popcorn stitches that edge the rim and brim. Designed by Mari Lynn Patrick.

SIZES
Instructions are written for one size.

KNITTED MEASUREMENTS
- Head circumference 20"/51cm
- Depth 8"/20.5cm

MATERIALS
- 2 1¾oz/50g balls (each approx 110yd/100m) of Lion Brand Yarn *Incredible* (nylon) in #206 Autumn Leaves (5)
- Size K/10½ (7mm) crochet hook *or size to obtain gauge*

GAUGE
- 13 hdc and 10 hdc rnds to 4"/10cm over hdc (in back loop) pat st using size K/10½ (7mm) hook. *Take time to check gauge.*

STITCH GLOSSARY
hdc4tog
(Yo and draw up a loop) 4 times in the same st, yo and pull through all loops on hook.

HAT
Beg at rim edge (above the brim), firmly chain 58 to measure 20"/51cm. Join with sl st to first ch to form ring.

Rnd 1 (popcorn pat) Ch 2 (counts as 1 hdc), skip first ch, *work hdc4tog in next ch, ch 1, skip 1 ch; rep from *, end hdc4tog in the last ch—58 sts. Join with sl st in ch-2.

Rnd 2 Ch 4, work 1 tr in each st across—58 tr. Join with sl st in top of ch-4.

Rnd 3 Ch 2, working in back loops only, work even on 58 hdc. Join with sl st in ch-2.

Rnd 4 Rep rnd 2.

Rnd 5 Ch 2, working in back loops only, [dec 1 hdc, 1 hdc in each of next 5 sts] 8 times—50 sts. Join.

Rnd 6 Ch 2, working in back loops only, [1 hdc in each of next 8 sts, dec 1 hdc] 5 times—45 sts. Join.

Rnd 7 Ch 2, working in back loops only, [1 hdc in each of next 7 sts, dec 1 hdc] 5 times—40 sts. Join.

Rnd 8 Ch 2, working in back loops only, [1hdc in each of next 6 sts, dec 1 hdc] 5 times—35 sts. Join.

Rnd 9 Ch 2, working in back loops only,

[1 hdc in each of next 5 sts, dec 1 hdc] 5 times—30 sts. Join.

Rnd 10 Ch 2, working in back loops only, [1 hdc in each of next 3 sts, dec 1 hdc] 6 times—24 sts. Join.

Rnd 11 Working in both loops, ch 2, [1 hdc in each of next 2 sts, dec 1 hdc] 6 times—18 st. Join.

Rnd 12 Working in both loops, ch 2, [1 hdc in next st, dec 1 hdc] 6 times—12 sts. Join.

Rnd 13 Working in both loops, ch 2, [dec 1 hdc] 6 times—6 sts. Fasten off.

BRIM

Return to the lower beg chain edge.

Rnd 1 Join yarn to beg of rnd, ch 1 and work 58 sc evenly around. Join with sl st to first sc.

Rnd 2 Ch 1, 2 sc in next sc, [1 sc in next sc, 2 sc in each of next 6 sc] 8 times, 2 sc in last sc—108 sts. Join.

Rnd 3 Ch 1, work even on 108 sc. Join.

Rnd 4 Ch 2, *hdc4tog in first st, ch 1, skip 1 st, 1 hdc in next st, ch 1, skip 1 st; rep from * to end.

Rnd 5 Ch 1, work 1 sc in each st and ch 1 to end. Fasten off.

■◀■■▭

Two strands of a fine mohair in light and dark shades are combined to make this "hat structured" cloche. A full detachable flower is sewn on with a decorative button center. Designed by Mari Lynn Patrick.

SIZES

Instructions are written for one size.

KNITTED MEASUREMENTS

■ Head circumference (above the rim) 21"/53cm

■ Depth 8¾"/22cm

MATERIALS

■ 2 ⅞oz/25g balls (each approx 109 yd/100m) each of Le Fibre Nobile/ Plymouth Yarns *Imperiale Super Kid Mohair* (mohair/polyamide) in #4123 lt green (A) and #4122 dk green (B) **④**

■ Sizes D/3, G/6 and I/9 (3, 4.5 and 5.5mm) crochet hooks *or size to obtain gauge*

■ Decorative leaf button from www. a fabric place.com

GAUGE

8 sts and 7 rows/rnds to 3"/7.5cm over sc/dc row pat using 2 strands of yarn held tog and size I/9 (5.5mm) crochet hook. *Take time to check gauge.*

Notes

1 Two balls of each color will make the hat as pictured here. To make a cap with only the flower (and no brim), only one ball of each color is needed.

2 Work with 1 strand of A and B held tog, unless stated otherwise.

CLOCHE

Beg at the rim edge (above the brim), using 1 strand A and B held tog, with size I/9 (5.5mm) hook, firmly chain 60, to measures approx 20"/51cm. Join with sl st to form ring, being careful not to twist the chain.

Rnd 1 Ch 1, work 1 sc in each ch—60 sts. Join with sl st to first sc.

Rnd 2 Ch 3 (counts as 1 dc), skip the first st, 1 dc in each of the next 8 sts, *2 dc in next st, 1 dc in each of next 9 sts rep from *, end 2 dc in last st—66 sts. Join with sl st to ch 3.

Rnd 3 Ch 1, work 1 sc in each st around, join with sl st to first sc.

Rnd 4 Ch 3 (counts as 1 dc), skip the first sc and dc in each sc to end. Join with sl st to ch- 3.

Rep rnds 3 and 4 3 times more. Piece measures approx 3½"/9cm from beg.

Rnd 11 Ch 1, *work 4 sc, dec 1 sc (over next 2 sts); rep from * 10 times more—55 sts. Join.

Rnd 12 Ch 3, *work 2 dc, dec 1 dc (over next 2 sts), work 1 dc; rep from *, end last rep with dec 1 dc—44 sts. Join.

Rnd 13 Ch 1, *work 2 sc, dec 1 sc; rep from * to end—33 sts. Join.

Rnd 14 Ch 3, work even in dc on 33 sts. Join.

Rnd 15 Ch 1, *work 1 sc, dec 1 sc; rep from * to end—22 sts. Join.

Rnd 16 Ch 1, [dec 1 sc] 11 times—11 sts. Join.

Rnd 17 Ch 1, work even in sc on 11 sts. Join.

Rnd 18 Ch 1, [dec 1 sc] 5 times, sc in last st. Cut yarn leaving a long end. Draw through the sts at top to close hole neatly.

Join 1 strand A and B to the other side of ch at the beg of the cloche using size I/9 (5.5mm) hook.

Rnd 1 Ch 3, work 1 dc in first ch (for 1 st inc), *2 dc in next ch, 1 dc in each of next 2 ch; rep from * to last ch, work 2 dc in last ch– 82 sts. Join.

Rnd 2 Ch 1, work even in sc on 82 sts. Join.

Rnd 3 Ch 3, work even in dc on 82 sts. Join.

Rnd 4 Ch 1, work even in sc on 82 sts. Join and fasten off.

Center

Using 1 strand only of color B and size D/3 (3mm) hook, ch 8, join with sl st to first ch to form ring.

Rnd 1 Ch 1, work 16 sc into ring, join with sl st to first sc.

Rnd 2 Ch 5 (counts as 1 dc and ch 2), skip next sc, [1 dc in next sc, ch 2, skip 1 sc] 7 times, join with sl st to 3rd ch of ch-5. There are 8 ch-2 spaces.

Rnd 3 Sl st into ch-2 space, ch 1, work (1 sc, 1 hdc, 1 dc, 1 hdc, 1 sc) into each of the 8 ch-2 spaces, join with sl st to first sc. Fasten off.

Using 1 strand each A and B held tog and size G/6 (4.5mm) hook, ch 5, join with sl st to first ch to form ring.

Rnd 1 Ch 1, work 10 sc into ring, join with sl st to first sc.

Rnd 2 Ch 1, work 1 sc in each sc around, join with sl st to first sc.

Rnd 3 Ch 2 (counts as 1 hdc), skip the first sc, work 2 hdc in each of the next 9 sc, then, 1 hdc into the first sc, sl st into 2nd ch of the ch-2.

Rnd 4 *Ch 2, working into the front loops only of each hdc around, work 2 hdc in each of the next 3 hdc, ch 2, sl st in (front loop of) next hdc; rep from * 4 times more placing the last sl st into 2nd ch of the ch-2 at beg of previous rnd—5 petals made.

Rnd 5 Working behind each petal of previous rnd and into back loops only of each hdc on the 3rd rnd, sl st into first 2 hdc, *ch 4, work 2 dtr into each of the next 3 hdc, ch 4, sl st into next hdc; rep from * 3 times more, ch 4, 2 dtr into next hdc, 2 dtr into 2nd ch of ch 2 at beg of the 3rd rnd, 2 dtr into next hdc, ch 4, sl st into next hdc. Fasten off, leaving long ends. Sew flower center in B to center of outer flower using button at center, sew flower to hat as shown.

AVIATOR HELMET
Wild blue yonder

Easy double crochet mesh forms this helmet design in elegant wool and angora "lush" blend yarn. Braids trim and anchor the base and form the ties in this design by Margarita Mejia.

SIZES

Instructions are written for one size.

KNITTED MEASUREMENTS

- Head circumference 20"/51 cm
- Depth 7¼"/18.5 cm

MATERIALS

- 2 1¾oz/50g balls (each approx 124yd/114m) of Classic Elite Yarns *Lush* (wool/angora) in #4407 thistle (4)
- Size G/6 (4.5mm) crochet hook *or size to obtain gauge*

GAUGE

5 mesh pats and 7 rnds to 4"/10cm over dc mesh pat using size G/6 (4.5mm) crochet hook. *Take time to check gauge.*

HELMET

Beg at top edge, ch 5, join with sl st to first ch to form ring.

Rnd 1 Work 12 sc in ring, join with sl st to first sc.

Rnd 2 Ch 4 (counts as 1 dc and ch 1), *1 dc in next sc, ch 1; rep from * around, join with sl st to 3rd ch of ch-4.

Rnd 3 Ch 3 (counts as 1 dc), 2 dc in first ch-1 space, *3 dc in next ch-1 space; rep from * around, join to top of ch-3—twelve 3-dc (groups) or mesh.

Rnds 4 and 5 Rep rnd 3.

Inc rnd 6 Ch 3, 2 dc in first ch-1 space, *(3 dc, ch 1, 3 dc) in next ch-1 space (for inc), 3 dc in next ch-1 space; rep from * 4 times more, inc in last ch-1 space—18 mesh.

Rnds 7-9 Work even on 18 mesh.

Inc rnd 10 Ch 3, 2 dc in first ch-1 space, *3 dc in next ch-1 space, inc in next ch-1 space, 3 dc in next ch-1 space; rep from * 4 times more, 3 dc in next ch-1 space, inc in last ch-1 space—24 mesh.

Rnds 11-14 Work even on 24 mesh.

Work earflaps

Rnd 15 Ch 3, 2 dc in first ch-1 space, work 4 more mesh, turn.

Next row Ch 3, 2 dc in first ch-1 space, work 3 more mesh, turn.

Next row Ch 3, 2 dc in first ch-1 space, work 2 more mesh, turn.

Next row Ch 3, 2 dc in first ch-1 space, work 1 more mesh, turn.

Last row Ch 3, 2 dc in first ch-1 space. Fasten off. Skip 5 mesh (for back of helmet), re-join yarn and work the 2nd earflap as for the first, do not fasten off at end.

Working around the entire lower edge of helmet, work 3 rnds of sc evenly around lower edge. Cut 12 strands of yarn to fit the 27"/68.5 cm around the lower edge of helmet plus several extra inches/cm for braiding. Braid tog and sew braid around lower edge of helmet. Cut 12 strands of yarn 25"/63.5 cm long and attach with a knot for braid tie to earflap tip. Braid and knot. Trim ends.

This cap design is crocheted in an all-over chain stitch that resemble, fishing net. It is stabilized by working into the center chain instead of the chain arch. A quick slip stitch round worked at the very end gives the cap an adjustable fit. Designed by Doris Chan.

SIZES

Instructions are written for one size.

KNITTED MEASUREMENTS

- Head circumference 21"/53 cm
- Depth 7"/18 cm

MATERIALS

- 1 1¾oz/50g hank (each approx 109yd/100m) of Cherry Tree Hill *Possum Prints Worsted* (wool/possum) in country garden (**4**)
- Size H/8 (5mm) crochet hook *or size to obtain gauge*

GAUGE

One ch-5 to 1¼"/3 cm and 8 rnds to 4"/10cm over chain mesh pat using size H/8 (5mm) crochet hook. *Take time to check gauge.*

Note The final sl st rnd is designed to pull the lower edge in to fit desired head size.

CAP

Rnd 1 Beg at crown edge, ch 4. Work 1 hdc in 4th ch from hook, then [ch 1, hdc] in same ch, sc in 2nd ch of ch-4 (to count as beg arch), turn. There are 6 ch-sps.

Rnd 2 (WS) Ch 1, sc in beg ch-sp, [ch 5, sc in next ch-sp] 5 times, ch 3, hdc in beg sc (to count as beg arch), turn.
There are 6 arches.

Rnd 3 (RS) Ch 1, sc in beg arch, [ch 5, sc in next sc, ch 5, sc in 3rd ch of next arch] 11 times, ch 3, hdc in beg sc, turn—12 arches.

Rnd 4 Ch 1, sc in beg arch, ch 5, sc in 3rd

ch of next arch, [ch 5, sc in next sc, ch 5, sc in 3rd ch of next arch, ch 5, sc in 3rd ch of next arch] 5 times, ch 5, sc in last sc, ch 3, hdc in beg sc, turn—18 arches.

Rnd 5 Ch 1, sc in beg arch, [ch 5, sc in 3rd ch of next arch] twice, *ch 5, sc in next sc, [ch 5, sc in 3rd ch of next arch] 3 times; rep from * 4 times more, ch 5, sc in last sc, ch 3, hdc in beg sc, turn—24 arches.

Rnds 6-13 Ch 1, sc in beg arch, [ch 5, sc in 3rd ch of next arch] 23 times, ch 3, hdc in beg sc, turn.

Rnd 14 Ch 1, sc in beg arch, [ch 3, sc in 3rd ch of next arch] 23 times, ch 3, sl st in beg sc, turn.

Rnd 15 Ch 1, [2 sc in next arch, sc in next sc] 24 times, sl st in beg sc, turn—72 sc.

Rnd 16 Sl st in each sc around, adjusting tension to fit desired head size, sl st in beg sl st. Fasten off.

Circle in the square

Single crocheted squares are laid out, domino-style, to form the top of this beret worked in pastels and heather color combinations. Triangles fill out the hexagonal shape and a ridged band fits the head in this design by Linda Medina.

SIZES

Instructions are written for one size.

KNITTED MEASUREMENTS

- Diameter 11"/28cm
- Depth (to center) 7"/18cm

MATERIALS

- 2 1¾oz/50 skeins (each approx 100yd/91m) of Knit One Crochet Too *Parfait Swirls* (wool) in #CL4222 pink heather (A) (4)
- 1 3½oz/100g skein (each approx 218yd/200m of Knit One Crochet Too *Parfait Solids* (wool) in #1289 pink (B) (4)
- Size G/6 (4.5mm) crochet hook *or size to obtain gauge*
- Elastic thread (optional)

GAUGE

One domino square is 3"/7.5 cm square using size G/6 (4.5mm) crochet hook. *Take time to check gauge.*

BERET

DOMINO SQUARE

(make 2)

With A, ch 24.

Row 1 Work 1 sc in 2nd ch from hook, 1 sc in each of next 9 ch, draw up a loop in next 3 ch, yo and draw through all 4 loops on hook (for dec), 1 sc in each of next 10 ch, ch 1, turn on this and all foll rows.

Row 2 Work 1 sc in each of 9 sc, work dec over center 3 sc, 1 sc in last 9 sc.

Row 3 Work 1 sc in each of 8 sc, work dec, 1 sc in last 8 sc.

Row 4 Work 1 sc in each of 7 sc, work dec, 1 sc in last 7 sc.

Row 5 Work 1 sc in each of 6 sc, work dec, 1 sc in last 6 sc.

Row 6 Work 1 sc in each of 5 sc, work dec, 1 sc in last 5 sc.

Row 7 Work 1 sc in each of 4 sc, work dec, 1 sc in last 4 sc. Cut A.

Row 8 Change to B and work 1 sc in each of 3 sc, work dec, 1 sc in last 3 sc.

Row 9 With B, work 1 sc in each of 2 sc, work dec, 1 sc in last 2 sc.

Row 10 With B, sc in first sc, work dec, sc in last sc.

Row 11 With B, draw up a loop in each sc, yo and through all 4 loops on hook. Fasten off.

TRIANGLE

(make 4)

With A, ch 17.

Row 1 Work 1 sc in 2nd ch from hook, 1 sc in each of next 12 ch, work dec, ch 1, turn on this and all foll rows.

Row 2 Work 11 sc, work dec.

Row 3 Work 9 sc, work dec.

Row 4 Work 7 sc, work dec.

Row 5 Work 5 sc, work dec.

Row 6 Work 3 sc, work dec.

Row 7 Work 1 sc, work dec.

Row 8 Work 1 sc, sl st in next sc.

Row 9 Work 1 sc. Fasten off.

ASSEMBLY

Foll layer diagram, assemble beret and sl st the pieces tog on the WS. Block lightly to measurements.

RIBBED BAND

With B, ch 8.

Row 1 Work 1 sc in 2nd ch from hook and next 6 ch, ch 1, turn.

Row 2 Working in back loops only, work 7 sc. Ch 1, turn. Rep row 2 until piece measures 20"/51 cm (or desired length to fit around hook). Sew the ribbed band, chain edge to last row, to form a circle. Then, cont along the rows of the circle, work 96 sc evenly spaced around the rib band. Join and ch 1, do not turn, but cont to work in rnds.

Rnd 1 *Work 1 sc in each of 11 sc, 2 sc in next sc; rep from * around—104 sc. Join and ch 1.

Rep rnd 1 for 8 times more—168 sc. Do not fasten off yarn.

FINISHING

Pin the band to the beret top. With band edge facing, sl st the band to the beret top using working B yarn. Join A to the beret top outer edge and working from left to right, work 1 backwards sc in each sc around. If desired, weave several strands of elastic through the ribbed band to fit.

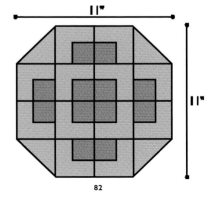

11" 11"

CAP WITH POPCORNS

Blueberry beanie

This miniature cap sits on top of the head and is fashioned with pretty popcorns and openwork shells. Designed by Doris Chen using a blueberry shade of sport weight wool.

SIZES
Instructions are written for one size.

KNITTED MEASUREMENTS
■ Head circumference 19"/48cm
■ Depth 6"/15cm

MATERIALS
■ 1 1¾oz/50g ball (each approx 116yd/107m) of Dale of Norway *Falk* (wool) in #5545 blue (4)
■ Size G/6 (4.5mm) crochet hook or *size to obtain gauge*

GAUGE
14 sc and 2 rows/rnds to 4"/10cm and one pat rep to 1¾"/4.5cm.
Take time to check gauge.

STITCH GLOSSARY
The pat st consists of 1 (WS) row of popcorns then 1 (RS) row of shells that is turned but worked in joined rnds.

Popcorn (PC)
(Work 4 dc) in one st, drop loop on hook, insert hook from front to back into first dc of 4-dc group, pick up dropped loop and pull through. Popcorn should "pop" to the opposite side (RS) as you work.

Shell
(Work dc, ch 1, dc, ch 1, dc) all in one st.

CAP
Beg at crown edge, ch 4. Join with sl st to form ring.

Rnd 1 (RS) Ch 4, [dc, ch 1] 11 times into ring, sl st to 3rd ch of beg ch, turn.

Rnd 2 (WS) Ch 1, sc in same st as joining, [ch 3, pc in next dc, ch 3, sc in next dc] 6 times, ending last rep with sl st (instead of sc)in beg sc—6 popcorns. Turn.

Rnd 3 Ch 4, [sc in top of sc, ch 1, shell in next sc, ch 1] 5 times, sc in top of last pc, ch 1, (dc, ch 1, dc, ch 1) in same st as beg, sl st in 3rd ch of beg ch—6 shells. Turn.

Rnd 4 Ch 1, sc in same st as joining, [ch 3, pc in dc ch 3, sc in next dc, ch 3, pc in next sc, ch 3, sc in next dc] 6 times, ending with omit last sc and sl st in beg sc— 12 popcorns. Turn.

Rnd 5 Ch 4, dc in same st as joining, [ch 1, sc in top of next pc, ch 1, shell in next sc] 11 times, ch 1, sc in top of last pc, ch 1, dc in same st as beg, ch 1, sl st in 3rd ch of beg ch—12 shells. Turn.

Rnd 6 Ch 1, sc in same st as joining, [ch 3, pc in next sc, ch 3, skip next dc, sc in next dc] 12 times, ending with omit last sc, sl st in beg sc, turn.

Rnds 7-12 Rep rnds 5 and 6 3 times. Cap measures approx 5"/12.5cm.

Rnd 13 Ch 1, sc in same st as joining, [2 sc in next ch-3 arch, sc in top of pc, 2 sc in next ch-3 arch, sc in next sc] 12 times, ending with omit last sc, do not turn— 72 sc.

Rnd 14 Pm to mark beg of rnd and ch 1, work even in sc around, end by join with sl st to first sc.

Rnds 15-18 Rep rnd 14. Fasten off.

CLASSIC CLOCHE

See scallops

This lightweight yet full-bodied wool yarn is worked in half-double crochet to give this cloche a slouchy charm. Designed by Kathy Merrick with a pretty openwork scallop pattern lace band circling the crown.

STITCH GLOSSARY

Dec 1 hdc

Yo hook and insert hook in next st, yo and pull up a loop, yo and insert hook in next st, yo and pull up a loop, yo and pull through all 5 loops.

Picot

Ch 3, sl st in third ch from hook.

CLOCHE

LACE BAND

Ch 25.

Row 1 Work 1 hdc in 3rd ch from hook, 1 hdc in each of next 5 ch, ch 6, skip 5 ch, 1 sc in next ch, ch 6, skip 5 ch, 1 hdc in each of last 6 ch, turn.

Row 2 Ch 2 (does not count as 1 hdc), work 6 hdc, Ch 4, sc in ch-6 loop, Ch 5, sc in ch-6 loop, Ch 4, work 6 hdc, turn.

Row 3 Ch 2, work 6 hdc, ch 1, make picot, ch 1, skip next ch-4 loop, 9 hdc in ch-5 loop, ch 1, make picot, ch 1, skip next ch-4 loop, work 6 hdc, turn.

Row 4 Ch 2, work 6 hdc, ch 6, 1 sc in the 5th hdc of 9-hdc group, ch 6, work 6 hdc, turn.

Row 5 Rep row 2.
Row 6 Rep row 3.

Rep rows 4-6 until lace band measures 21½"/55cm from beg. Sl st the beg ch and last row tog to form the band.

CROWN

Rnd 1 From RS, join yarn to top of lace band and work 102 hdc evenly around, join with sl st to first hdc.

Rnd 2 Working in back loops only, work even in hdc around. Do not join to first hdc, but cont to work in a spiral. Place yarn marker to mark beg of rnd.

Rnd 3 *Dec 1 hdc, work 10 hdc; rep from *, end dec 1 hdc, work 4 hdc—93 hdc.

Rnd 4 *Dec 1 hdc, work 9 hdc; rep from *, end dec 1 hdc, work 3 hdc—84 hdc.

Rnd 5 *Dec 1 hdc, work 8 hdc; rep from *, end dec 1 hdc, work 2 hdc—75 hdc.

Rnd 6 *Work 7 hdc, dec 1 hdc; rep from *, end work 3 hdc—67 hdc.

Rnd 7 *Dec 1 hdc, work 6 hdc; rep from *, end dec 1 hdc, work 1 hdc—58 hdc.

Rnd 8 *Work 5 hdc, dec 1 hdc; rep from * end dec 1 hdc—49 hdc.

Rnd 9 *Dec 1 hdc, work 4 hdc; rep from *, end work 1 hdc—41 hdc.

Rnd 10 *Work 3 hdc, dec 1 hdc; rep from *, end work 1 hdc—33 hdc.

Rnd 11 *Dec 1 hdc, work 2 hdc; rep from *, end work 1 hdc—25 hdc.

Rnd 12 *Work 1 hdc, dec 1 hdc; rep from *, end work 1 hdc—17 hdc.

Rnd 13 [Dec 1 hdc] 8 times, work 1 hdc—9 hdc.

Cut yarn leaving a long end. Pull through all rem sts, draw up tightly and secure.

BRIM

Rnd 1 From RS, join yarn to lower edge of lace band and work 102 hdc evenly around, join with sl st to first hdc.

Rnd 2 Working in back loop only, work even in hdc around. Do not join to first hdc, but cont to work in a spiral.

Rnd 3 *Work 2 hdc in next hdc (for inc), work 11 hdc; rep from *, end work 2 hdc in next hdc, work 5 hdc—111 hdc.

Rnd 4 *Work 12 hdc, 2 hdc in next hdc; rep from *, end work 6 hdc, work 2 hdc in last hdc—120 hdc.

Rnd 5 *Work 2 hdc in next hdc, work 13 hdc; rep from *, end work 2 hdc in next hdc, work 7 hdc—129 hdc.

Rnd 6 *Work 14 hdc, 2 hdc in next hdc; rep from *, work 8 hdc, work 2 hdc in last hdc—138 hdc.

Rnd 7 *Work 2 hdc in next hdc, work 15 hdc; rep from *, end with 2 hdc in next hdc, work 9 hdc—147 hdc.

Rnd 8 *Work 16 hdc, 2 hdc in next hdc; rep from *, end work 10 hdc, 2 hdc in last hdc—156 hdc.

Rnd 9 *Work 2 hdc in next hdc, work 17 hdc; rep from *, end work 2 hdc in next hdc, work 11 hdc—165 hdc.

Rnd 10 *Work 18 hdc, 2 hdc in next hdc; rep from *, end work 12 hdc, 2 hdc in last hdc—174 hdc.

Rnd 11 *Work 2 hdc in next hdc, work 19 hdc; rep from *, end work 2 hdc in next hdc, work 13 hdc—183 hdc.

Rnd 12 *Work 20 hdc, 2 hdc in next hdc; rep from *, end work 14 hdc, 2 hdc in last hdc—192 hdc.

Rnd 13 Work even in hdc. Fasten off.

RESOURCES

Write to the yarn companies listed below for purchasing and mail-order information.

BERROCO, INC.
P.O. Box 367
Uxbridge, MA 01569
In Canada:
distributed by
S.R. Kertzer, Ltd.

BLUE SKY ALPACAS
PO Box 387
St. Francis, MN 55070

BROWN SHEEP COMPANY, INC.
100662 County Road 16
Mitchell, NE 69357
www.brownsheep.com

CHERRY TREE HILL
PO Box 659
Barton, VT 05822

CLASSIC ELITE YARNS
300 Jackson St., Bldg. #5
Lowell, MA 01852
classicelite@aol.com

DALE OF NORWAY, INC.
N16 W23390 Stoneridge Dr.
Suite A
Waukesha, WI 53188

DIAMOND YARN
9697 St. Laurent
Montreal, Quebec PQ H3L
2N1 and 155 Martin Ross,
Unit #3
Toronto, ON M3J 2L9

DMC
#10 Port Kearny
South Kearny, NJ 07032

FILATURA DI CROSA
distributed by
Tahki•Stacy Charles, Inc.
In Canada:
distributed by
Diamond Yarn

JCA, INC.
35 Scales Lane
Townsend, MA 01469

KARABELLA YARNS, INC.
1201 Broadway, Suite 311
New York, NY 10001
(212) 684-2665
arthurkarapetyan@aol.com

KNIT ONE CROCHET TOO
7 Commons Avenue, Suite 2
Windham, ME 04062

KNITTING FEVER, INC.
P.O. Box 502
Roosevelt, NY 11575

KOIGU WOOL DESIGNS
RR #1
Williamsford, ON N0H 2V0

LE FIBRE NOBILE
distributed by
Plymouth Yarn

LION BRAND YARN
34 West 15th Street
New York, NY 10011
www.lionbrand.com
In Canada:
distributed by
Domcord Belding
660 Denison St.
Markham, ON L3R 1C1

MUENCH YARNS
1323 Scott Street
Petaluma, CA 94954

NATURALLY
distributed by
S.R. Kertzer, Ltd.

NATURWOLLE
distributed by
Muench Yarns

NORO
distributed by
Knitting Fever, Inc.

PLYMOUTH YARN
P.O. Box 28
Bristol, PA 19007
www.plymouthyarn.com

REYNOLDS
distributed by JCA, Inc.

ROWAN YARNS
4 Townsend West, Unit 8
Nashua, NH 03063

S. CHARLES COLLEZIONE
distributed by
Tahki•Stacy Charles, Inc.

S.R. KERTZER, LTD.
105A Winges Road
Woodbridge, ON L4L 6C2
(800) 263-2354
www.kertzer.com

TAHKI•STACY CHARLES, INC.
70-30 80th Street
Bldg. 36
Ridgewood, NY 11385

UK RESOURCES

*Not all yarns used in this
book are available in
the UK. For yarns not
available, make a
comparable substitute or
contact the US manufacturer
for purchasing and
mail-order information.*

COLINETTE YARNS
Units 2-5
Banwy Workshops
Llanfair Caereinion
Powys SY21 0SG
Tel: 01938-810128

DEBBIE BLISS
distributed by Designer Yarns
Newbridge Interbrough
Estate
Unit 8-10, Pitt Street
Keighley, West Yorkshire
BD21 4PQ

JAEGER HANDKNITS
Green Lane Mill
Holmfirth
West Yorks HD7 1RW
Tel: 01484-680050

ROWAN YARNS
Green Lane Mill
Holmfirth
West Yorks HD7 1RW
Tel: 01484-681881

Editorial Director
TRISHA MALCOLM

Art Director
CHI LING MOY

Executive Editor
CARLA S. SCOTT

Book Manager
ERICA SMITH

Graphic Designers
SHEENA THOMAS
CAROLINE WONG

Instructions Editor
MARI LYNN PATRICK

Yarn Editor
VERONICA MANNO

Production Manager
DAVID JOINNIDES

Photography
RADIUS PICTURES

Photo Stylist
LAURA MAFFEO

Technical Illustrations
MATT DOJNY

President, Sixth&Spring Books
ART JOINNIDES

LOOK FOR THESE OTHER TITLES IN THE VOGUE KNITTING ON THE GO! SERIES...

■

BABY BLANKETS

BABY BLANKETS TWO

BABY GIFTS

BABY KNITS

BABY KNITS TWO

BAGS & BACKPACKS

BEGINNER BASICS

CAPS & HATS

CAPS & HATS TWO

CHUNKY KNITS

CHUNKY SCARVES & HATS

CROCHET BASICS

CROCHETED SCARVES

FELTING

KIDS KNITS

MITTENS & GLOVES

PILLOWS

PONCHOS

SCARVES

SCARVES TWO

SOCKS

SOCKS TWO

TEEN KNITS

TODDLER KNITS

VESTS

VINTAGE KNITS

WEEKEND KNITS